PROFILES IN INDEPENDENCE:
STARTING A HOME-BASED BUSINESS

By Gene E. Pike
M.B.A., C.P.A., C.M.A.

Sherwood Publishing, Valrico, Florida

PROFILES IN INDEPENDENCE:

STARTING A HOME-BASED BUSINESS

By: Gene E. Pike

Published By:
Sherwood Publishing
1906 Canyonwood Ct.
Valrico, Fl 33594

Publisher's Cataloging in Publication Data
Pike, Gene E.
Profiles In Independence: Starting A Home-Based Business
p. cm.
Bibliography:P.
Includes Index
1. Home-Based Businesses
2. Computers
3. Marketing
4. Accounting

ISBN 0-9631724-0-9: $14.95 Softcover

ABOUT THE AUTHOR

Gene E. Pike, MBA, CPA, CMA, is the President of Gene Pike & Associates, Inc., a consulting firm specializing in the development of equipment leasing seminars and personal computer software. A nationally known author and trainer in the leasing industry, Gene has conducted over 250 seminars with more than 7,000 participants.

Married, two children, and 32 years old, Gene left the financial security of corporate management in GTE Corporation in late 1983 to form his own company. In his last assignment, as the Financial Education Program Manager at the GTE Advanced Management Development Center, Gene realized a potential market niche existed in marketing specialized corporate training in Computer Leasing. Gene Pike & Associates, Inc., currently offers Lease Negotiations Workshops for lessees and Lease Marketing Skills Workshops for leasing companies.

Gene gained his financial expertise and experience in computer leasing while in financial management at GTE Data Services, Inc. He offered a unique combination of practical leasing experience, an academic background in finance and accounting, and teaching experience gained in corporate education and teaching in the College of Business at the University of South Florida.

Academically, Gene has a degree in Finance from Brigham Young University and a Masters Degree in Business Administration (MBA) with a concentration in Accounting from the University of Tampa. He is also a Certified Public Accountant (CPA) licensed in Florida and is a Certified Management Accountant (CMA) through the National Institute of Management Accounting.

With an entrepreneurial drive since his college days, Gene and his wife Sandy, are also currently involved in the ownership of residential and commercial real estate including apartments, homes, offices, and a self-service car wash.

Sandy Pike, editor of this book, earned a Finance Degree from the University of South Florida and worked as an Internal Revenue Service (IRS) Auditor before forming an accounting and tax preparation partnership with another IRS Auditor. After selling her share of the accounting firm, Sandy was the Fiscal Manager for a county wide agency until starting to work full time with Gene.

DISCLAIMER

Hopefully this book will provide some encouragement and ideas in helping you decide if you want to start a home-based business. If you have already made that decision, some of the ideas and marketing thoughts might help get you a few extra customers or help keep your business on an even keel. If the book does help, I will be glad to take some of the credit for your success.

If you are broke and looking for someone to blame, just remember I am a poor Florida consultant. This book is not intended to provide legal advice nor specific tax advice. I have tried to make it as accurate and as practical as I can, but neither the author nor Sherwood Publishing shall be liable for any errors or omissions, or any loss or damages, directly or indirectly, alleged to be caused by information contained in this book.

ACKNOWLEDGMENT

A number of people contributed to the writing of this book, especially my wife Sandy, who had to read and edit and edit and edit all my thoughts. She was a tremendous help in getting this book into a finished format. Sandy also wrote the insurance section based on her experience in negotiating a health insurance program for the county wide agency for which she worked as the Fiscal Manager.

Even my son, Shane, got drafted into reviewing the manuscript. As a senior in Accounting at the University of Florida, his editing came with a price tag. I have to mention that the U of F football team won the SEC (Southeastern Conference) this year. Go Gators! If you are a Florida State (Seminole) fan, I apologize, but you will have to put the book back on the shelf.

To the entrepreneurs who contributed to the profiles, my appreciation. It takes a lot of courage to start a home-based business and even more dedication to make a business succeed. To Don Pate, Enrolled Agent, who reviewed the accounting and tax section, thanks. It is a lot of work to stay current on tax law and I wanted to make sure we got it right. To Mike Lovchuk, who reviewed the insurance chapter, our thanks and continued success in your insurance agency. To all my other friends who have read different sections, thanks for the comments and observations. I am sorry my tennis game has not been up to par lately. I told them I was working on a book, and they all thought I had been goofing off again. Gene working? Not likely!

Thanks again to all the PROFILES:

Mary Seiferd and Jan Hudgins	Merrill Nipper
Michele Harber	Nico Pavan
Dennison Osborne	Don Pressler
Lori Reeves	Chris Cook
Frank and Sue Bordas	Steve Madson
Gordon Hill	Brenda Saling
Sheryl Nicholson	Skip Moore
Donald B. Pate	Paul Walsh
Bill Pinciotti	

STARTING A HOME-BASED BUSINESS

TABLE OF CONTENTS

INTRODUCTION

As I began the planning process that led to the writing of this book, I must admit I hadn't originally planned to write a book. I was simply looking for a book featuring companies that had actually been started at home and how the owners had handled all the decisions and challenges which face a new business.

I found a lot of books about starting a business, but most were academic and went into great detail about the difference between regular corporations, 1120S corporations, and Schedule C businesses and all the tax considerations in starting a business. A good business foundation is important, but I was looking for encouragement. I wanted some success stories, individuals who had actually had the courage to leave a corporate environment and the security of knowing (or at least planning on) that paycheck being there every two weeks.

I wanted to know the risks as well as the potential rewards, the right and wrong decisions and the insecurities associated with being responsible for your own future. It is easy to blame "*the company*" when things are not going well, but who do you blame when "**you**" are the company.

Since I did not find what I was looking for, I decided to interview a cross section of individuals who had actually started their own home-based businesses. I interviewed professionals who had left secure well-paying corporate environments, as well as homemakers and young entrepreneurs. The result is **PROFILES IN INDEPENDENCE: STARTING A HOME-BASED BUSINESS.**

The intent in **PROFILES IN INDEPENDENCE** is not just to discuss basic business concepts in finance, accounting, and marketing, but to show how different individuals started with a business concept (or dream), translated the concept into specific business steps (a Business Plan) and took the first, and then second and third steps which led to being their own boss (Implementation).

Throughout the book, I have drawn from indepth interviews with successful home-based business owners, as well as my experience in heading my own home-based business to develop basic lessons, steps, and business **truisms**.

Let me also express my appreciation to my wife, friends, and associates who contributed their time and energy in reviewing sections of this book and the entrepreneurs who had the courage to start their own home-based businesses and the willingness to share their experiences and lessons learned. All of these lessons were "paid for" as none of us made all the right decisions. Hopefully, we learned from our mistakes and they did not cost too much. Like all lessons, you can pick and choose the ones you like.

PERSONAL FREEDOM

Hopefully, this book will help you in making your decision to start a home-based business. I assume you are either thinking about it or have already decided to start a business or you would not be reading this book. If you've already made the decision, Congratulations! It is a tough decision to make, but from my experience and interviews with other home-based businesses profiled in this book, the personal freedom and satisfaction of being responsible for your own success or failure is well worth the risk.

Unlike Darby O'Gill and his search for the "little people," our dreams can become reality. We can find success based on our own terms and definition, and not defined by a pot of gold, or the car we drive, or the size of our home.

I started my own business at the end of 1983 when I was 32, married, had two children and was working in middle management for GTE Corporation. Was it a hard decision to leave? Most of my friends thought I was crazy. My dad was absolutely certain of it! In looking back, there have been ups and downs, months of working long hours and traveling every week followed by periods of insecurity wondering when that next assignment would be approved. Did I make the right decision? In 1989, during a period of insecurity and concern for the future, I went back to work for a large Fortune 500 company. The position fit perfectly with my professional expertise and experience and was within commuting distance of my home. I could not have written a better job description.

I was back in the corporate world. Working 8 to 5, suit and tie, briefcase, excellent benefits, good pay, and professional respect. I lasted 7 weeks before I resigned..........! I am not sure I am employable any more.   After eight years of self employment, independence and personal freedom becomes pretty important. Bureaucracy becomes an alien concept (Vice Presidential approval for an adding machine seems a bit too much).

Leaving home at 6:45 A.M. for an hour and ten minute commute and getting back at 6:30 P.M. becomes a strange and strangling way to live. To the home-based business, commute is what we do when we walk from the bedroom to the livingroom or spare bedroom (or both) which has been converted to an office.

To complete the story of my return to the corporate world, an hour and ten minute commute was really a little too much. I had originally planned to take a few months to get settled into the position and then buy a nice waterfront home close to corporate headquarters, due to the location of the company near Tampa Bay and the Gulf of Mexico. With our two sons in college, it was time for a sail boat, moonlight walks along the beach, tennis, and living the good life in "Margaritaville."

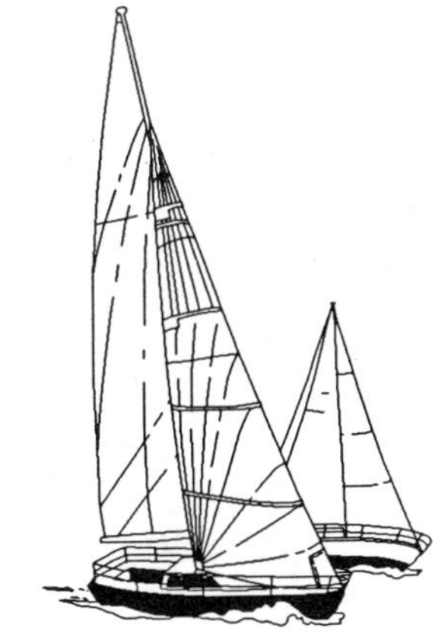

Just this last week, I read an article in the business section of the Tampa Tribune that the company had made the decision to concentrate on their core business and was liquidating the subsidiaries which the company had acquired during a ten year period of diversification. Included in the companies for sale was a $700 million portfolio of leases (primarily airplanes and transportation equipment) in which they had invested through their financial services subsidiary. As I read the last line, I mentally finished the sentence, *"which Gene Pike had been hired to manage, but since he only lasted seven weeks, he doesn't have to worry about not having a job, and what to do with an expensive waterfront home."* Corporate security is an illusion and "Margaritaville" is a town which only exists in a song!

This book is about personal freedom and quality of life. The freedom to live and enjoy life on your own terms. Work when you want to work without the regimentation of a clock or authority figure. It is not about getting rich (although if it happens it's OK). Hopefully, it is about helping you translate a business concept or dream to a workable business plan and giving you the encouragement to take one step at a time to make that dream a reality.

SELF-DISCIPLINE

If you will notice part of the title is **STARTING A HOME-BASED BUSINESS**. I want to stress that business and the concept of work go together. Personal freedom and quality of life does not automatically mean lots of leisure and recreation. One of the drawbacks to working out of your own home is that you have to schedule your own workload and do the work. I know this sounds like a funny drawback, but let me assure you there are lots of distractions.

As friends realize you are home during the day (they do not always equate the concept of home and work) you will suddenly get invitations for tennis, fishing, boating, golf and many other recreational activities. Well-meaning friends who are also self employed, on vacation, working alternating shifts, or are retired want to make sure you do not get bored and **do not get any work done.**

You must have the self-discipline to say **NO!** There is no "boss" to make you stay in your office and work. There is no clock you have to punch. There is only self-discipline and you have to exercise it. This does not mean you can not work based on your own schedule. If you go play tennis in the morning it may mean you have to work until midnight. That's OK, it's your business. That is why you work from home. In fact, do not tell your friends you will be working until midnight, let them think you play everyday, it is good for your ego. Let them be envious.

The greatest benefit of working from home is the flexibility to work and play when you want, but also remember you still have to pay the bills. The balance between the two is up to you. Paying the bills, by the way, might take a slight precedence and is the subject of the first chapter.

PERSONAL LIFESTYLES

As you assess your own lifestyle, you might also think in terms of whether a home-based business is right for you. If you measure life in terms of power, prestige, and all the business trappings that go with a corporate lifestyle there is no point in finishing the book. On the other hand, if you measure success in terms of family relationships, personal satisfaction from finishing a project, and having a balance between your personal and professional life then a home-based business might be just right for you.

If security is the number one priority in your life, I do not know what advice to offer. The corporate world in the last few years has certainly lost its luster as LBO's (Leveraged Buy Outs) in the 1980s, a pretty severe recession, the Savings & Loan Crisis, the Wall Street bloodletting, and the failure or merger of some the largest commercial banks in the country are contributing to massive layoffs of both clerical and the white collar work force. As I was writing this book, I read an article about the merger between Bank of America and Security Pacific Corporation to form one of the largest Bank holding companies in the world. Chemical Bank and Manufacturers Hanover also just merged as well as NCNB (North Carolina National Bank) and C&S (Citizens & Southern out of Atlanta). In the Business Week article, it talks about a $1 billion cost cutting goal with hundreds of branches and approximately 14,000 jobs to be eliminated.

If I was in corporate management or even a clerical position, articles like that would certainly make me feel insecure in corporate America! In fact, I can not think of a single business which guarantees a long term sense of security.

> A home-based business is no guarantee of a secure future, but at least you are in control of your own "insecurity."

If you can establish a lifestyle with which you are comfortable and then develop a home-based business which will support that lifestyle, that is the best security I know of. (Of course, I would have preferred rich parents.)

A home-based business probably will not make you a millionaire. But how many times have you heard a successful businessperson say, "*If only I had the time to relax?*" What is the tradeoff between financial success and personal satisfaction? What is the value of assets if you do not have the time to enjoy them? I do not know the answers, but I do know you would be a millionaire if you had a dollar every time one of your working friends sees you on the tennis court and says, "*If only I had your money!*"

If only they knew the truth!!!!

CHAPTER 1

PERSONAL
FINANCIAL PLANNING

This might be an odd chapter to start with, but working from home is not instant financial freedom. If you are already financially secure, skip this chapter and go on to the next. But, if you are like most of us, starting your own home-based business takes financial planning to ensure you can handle the transition period from that paycheck every two weeks to generating your own income.

TRUISM #1:   LIVE LIKE A SQUIRREL.

The key to personal financial planning and success in operating your home-based business is dependent on your ability to exercise a degree of financial self-discipline. The most acute insecurity you will feel in your home-based business (or even if you have a normal job), is the concern with financial security for the future.

I can not stress this point enough; it is amazing how we all have the capacity to spend exactly whatever cash is available. Whether it be an insurance settlement, a lump sum corporate retirement, or an inheritance, in just a few months or years it is all gone and we do not have a clue where the money went. Recently there was a lottery winner in the local newspaper who won a $5,000,000 Canadian lottery and went from instant wealth to bankruptcy in less than five years. I can not conceive how she did it. It is hard to believe that someone could spend that much money that fast. If you are thinking the IRS took a large share, you are wrong. The IRS was one of the creditors, she did not even pay the taxes on the lottery winnings.

A home-based business is the worst temptation of all, you must exercise self-control because there is no one else to do it for you and the cash flow that we generate is not consistent from month to month. In good months, as the cash flow exceeds our requirements, save the excess. In the lean months, draw against the accumulated savings to continue paying yourself a consistent amount or salary based on an annual financial budget we are going to develop in this chapter. If you can not exercise this self-control, do not even think about a home-based business unless you give the checkbook to your spouse or a partner who can.

Personally, this has never been a problem. I always assume if there are blank checks left at the end of the month there must be money to cover them!!!!

I know you are probably thinking personal financial planning is really basic and *LIVING LIKE A SQUIRREL* is a pretty simplistic Truism! It is basic and simplistic, but I assure you when you get that first **"big"** check you will immediately think about a new car or the vacation to Europe you have dreamed about (which you probably deserve because you have been working so hard).

You know I am telling the truth. During my last few years with GTE Corporation, I drove a brown 1977 Porsche 911S Targa. Every corporate executive needs one, and in addition, I love sports cars. As I evaluated, planned for, and decided to start my own corporate training business, I worried about the 911. It was getting older, had a few too many miles on it and I was concerned about unplanned maintenance expenses while trying to build my business. I decided to sell the Porsche and get a Honda. I did! I bought a brand new 1984 Honda Prelude. I picked blue since there were only three colors to choose from. It was a great car. I kept it four months!!!

My corporate financial training business started doing well right from the start. I had been the Financial Education Program Manager at the GTE Worldwide Management Development Center, teaching and developing corporate financial education courses. After resigning, I continued to teach the same courses as a consultant for GTE while also marketing financial training workshops to other companies. With a renewed sense of self confidence and **money** in the business account, I sold the Honda and purchased a brand new 1985 white Porsche 944 with matching white alloy wheels. I know exactly what it is like when those first "big" checks come in!!! Do you want me to also tell you about the month long trip to Europe?

As you are planning your monthly budget, you also need to think in terms of total debt as well as monthly payments. I have a friend, who, a few years back traded in two family cars on a new Cadillac. It was beautiful, and as we were admiring the gold trim and leather interior he made the remark, "*I saved $300 a month getting this car.*" I must have looked puzzled, because he went on to explain: One of the old cars had a payment of $325 a month with a balance of about $1,500 and the second car had a payment of $400 a month with a loan of about $4,500 remaining. By trading both cars in on the Cadillac, he only had to finance about $20,000 with a corresponding payment of $425 a month or $300 less than the combined $725 he had been paying on both the old cars. It made perfect sense, except while he saw the $300 monthly cash flow savings, all I saw was that he went from owing $6,000 with just a few payments left, to owing $20,000 with payments for the next five years.

Because he was now down to one car, it was not long before he realized he needed a second car, so he bought a friend's two year old Corvette. He financed it with a **BALLOON** loan. The loan was due, in full, in a year so he saved the monthly payments.

PERSONAL BUDGET

Now that we know we are going to develop a personal expense budget and live within that budget, we also need to project whether our home-based business and other investment income (interest, dividends, alimony, etc.) or income from a working spouse will support our lifestyle. If not, a **JOB** certainly looks better and better.

While we are talking about personal financial planning and budgeting, look in your wallet and count your credit cards.............. four, five, six, seven! You only need two. One for business and one for personal use. What are all the rest for? If you are counting a gas card, a furniture charge card, two Visa's, one MasterCard just in case you need it, Sears', Penney's, Macy's and the last you do not even recognize you have already got a credit card problem. Take them all out and put them in a drawer. If you can go without using them for three months, then cut them in half and get that outstanding balance paid off.

For most people, credit cards are extremely easy to lose control of. It is so easy to see something you would like and just whip out that credit card. If you are thinking, *"But, I never charge anything for myself,"* it's just as addictive if you are charging "impulse items" for your spouse or children. Does a four year old really need the latest pair of Air Jordan tennis shoes or designer play clothes? In fact, are you charging items because they need something, or to enhance your self-esteem.

Here is a two question litmus test to determine if you are a credit card "junkie." Do you get a cash advance from one card to pay the minimum monthly payment on another card? Do you have multiple credit cards and just pay the minimum payment on each? If you answered yes to either question, forget about a home-based business for awhile and get your personal finances in order. Start by cutting up those cards.

Back to my original point about only needing two cards. Get one general purpose charge card such as Visa or American Express and have it issued in your business name. You are still personally liable for the debt, but it will make accounting and taxes much easier since you will have a receipt for all your expenditures. A corporate credit card also appears very professional as you use it for business purposes. I have also found it is usually easier to use a credit card than a company check because with a company check you usually have to go through the same identification (driver's license, birthday, address, etc.) routine as with a personal check. Try not to use your business card for personal charges. Have a second general purpose charge card for your personal use. Preferably, have a different type of card for your personal charges so you do not mix them up. For example, have an American Express card for business and Visa or MasterCard for your personal use.

Now that we have taken care of our credit cards, it would be nice to know just where our money goes each month and how much we have available to support the startup and ongoing expenses of our home-based business. As you are beginning to think in terms of a personal budget and your current expenditures, keep in mind that going to a home-based business does minimize the overhead and operating expenses associated with both a start-up company and your personal finances. It

is surprising how expensive it is to establish an office in a normal rental environment. The next time you are driving and see a storefront office or retail store in a commercial strip center that has gone out of business, give a thought to the entrepreneur who just lost a significant investment in leasehold improvements, advertising, office furniture and equipment, supplies, inventory and employee wages. It will make you appreciate the ease and minimal risk associated with opening a home-based business.

From a personal standpoint, a home-based business also impacts your normal expenditures due to the change in your travel and work routine. While considering your budget try to consider the impact of the following potential savings:

POTENTIAL SAVINGS

* Automobile commuting costs including gas, repairs, insurance, and tolls. (These are difficult to project but if you want an estimate take your monthly commuting miles and multiply by about $ .24 a mile.)

* Restaurant lunches and snacks which are avoided. At a cost of $5-$10 a day depending on the part of the country you live in this equates to $100-$200 a month.

* Clothes and dry cleaning costs. As you make the transition from the "white collar" to the "open collar" workforce you will find knit shirts replacing white

shirts and suits. I have friends who are convinced I do not even own a suit and tie.

As you assess your financial requirements (you knew this part was coming) and the feasibility of starting a home-based business go ahead and fill in the following budget based on your own estimates. I have provided some sample numbers to get you started.

PERSONAL CASH FLOW (MONTHLY)

	EXAMPLE	YOURS
Housing Costs (Rent or mortgage)	$ 700	
Automobile Payment #1	250	
Automobile Payment #2		
Average Electric/Gas Bill	150	
Sewer, Water and Garbage	25	
Phone Bill	25	
Automobile Insurance	100	
Life/Health Insurance	50	
Automobile Gas/Maintenance	100	
Groceries/Food	300	
Visa/MasterCard/American Express	200	
Clothing	100	
School Expenses		
Entertainment	200	
Misc.		
TOTAL	$ 2,200	

Once you have developed a monthly budget, convert it to an annual cash flow which you need to meet in order to pay your bills. In our sample budget, a couple with two small children, a monthly expense of $2,200 is equal to an after-tax cash flow of $26,400. Keep in mind this is after-tax cash flow not earned income as we still need to pay social security and income taxes to derive the pretax income which we need to earn.

In developing your own cash flow, keep in mind the potential savings in monthly expenses as you convert to a home-based business. Using 1991 tax guidelines and a simple tax assumption of a standard deduction of $ 5,700 and 4 personal exemptions at $2,150 each, we have $14,300 in tax deductions which we will use in calculating our tax liability.

INCOME	SAMPLE	YOURS
AfterTax Cash Flow Required	$ 26,400	$
Less: Tax Deductions		
Standard Deduction (1991)	5,700	
Personal Deductions 4 @ $2,150	8,600	
Taxable Income	$ 12,100	$
Federal Income Taxes		
First $ 34,500 @ 15%	1,815	
Next $ 48,150 @ 28%		
Next $ Unlimited @ 31%		
Income Taxes	1,815	
AfterTax Cash + Income Taxes	$ 28,215	$
PreTax Cash Flow (Above ÷ by .8693 to reflect 13.07% Net Social Security Tax. See page 110 for calculations)	$ 32,457	$

We also have to consider social security, which on an after-tax basis is about 13.07% of our income assuming we are self-employed. (We will get into more detail about taxes and corporate structures in Chapter 5.) Based on the above assumptions, we can back into the projected level of income required by dividing the after-tax cash flow plus income taxes by (1 - 13.07% the effective after-tax social security rate). Depending on our personal or business income tax rate, the effective social security tax rate will change a little bit, but we are close enough to begin some preliminary personal financial planning.

In our sample family, the personal budget is about $32,457 a year, or $2,705 per month. In fact, this is probably not out of line for many American families. As we begin to assess the feasibility of our home-based business we need to determine the potential income based on some unit of productivity. In a generalized book, it is difficult to tailor the analysis to a specific business, but the most common billing or productivity measure in a small business is hours billed. If you are anticipating a service business, you may want to consider a job rate verses an hourly rate as a marketing strategy. In a later chapter on marketing, we will discuss billing strategies more thoroughly.

REASONABLENESS TEST

As an initial "reasonableness" test; the following table is based on the billing rate per hour needed to achieve our desired pretax income level after all expenses of operating the business. This is a key assumption; as we have not discussed the operating expenses you will incur in your home-based business, these billing rates may look artificially low.

The second consideration or assumption built into the table is the billing or productivity level you think you can achieve. For example, 52 weeks a year at 40 hours per week is a potential billing of 2,080 hours. In some companies this is also the projected billing level as a normal work week of 48 hours may be expected with the additional 8 hours of unbilled work offsetting holidays, vacation, sick time, ongoing professional training, and nonbilled administrative or marketing time.

In some cases, companies even have a minimum billing unit. For example, in many law firms a minimum of 15 minutes is billed for any client contact. If you call your attorney with a quick question and the conversation only lasts 2 minutes and you get a bill for $37.50, then one of two things occurred. Your attorney has a billing rate of $1,125 per hour or you just got billed for 15 minutes based on $150 an hour.

As you review the table, a 70% billing rate or 28 hours a week is probably not unreasonable, especially considering holidays and vacations. You will also be operating as a home-based business with an emphasis on marketing and trying to build a customer base during the first few years.

NET BILLING RATE PER HOUR

ANNUAL INCOME	80% BILLING (32hrs/week)	70% BILLING (28hrs/week)	60% BILLING (24hrs/week)
$ 20,000	$ 12.02	$ 13.74	$ 16.03
$ 30,000	$ 18.03	$ 20.60	$ 24.04
$ 40,000	$ 24.04	$ 27.47	$ 32.05
$ 50,000	$ 30.05	$ 34.34	$ 40.06
$ 60,000	$ 36.06	$ 41.21	$ 48.08
$ 70,000	$ 42.07	$ 48.08	$ 56.09
$ 80,000	$ 48.08	$ 54.95	$ 64.10

In many service oriented home-based businesses, net and gross billing rates are almost the same. For example, consulting is usually invoiced based on an hourly or daily rate plus expenses incurred. If this is the case, unbilled operating expenses should be nominal. In one of the **PROFILES IN INDEPENDENCE** which we will be reviewing, this is exactly the case as all operating expenses are rebilled. The only expenses incurred and not rebilled are overhead items such as accounting/tax preparation fees for the business, expenses incurred to prepare and print marketing brochures, and any advertising/marketing expenses.

As you compare your own financial budget with the type of business service you plan to offer, you can quickly begin to assess whether your home-based business is a viable offering. For example, if you are a corporate financial professional thinking about a home-based accounting and tax preparation business, in my area of the country small accounting firms are charging in the area of $30 an hour for staff preparation of monthly financial statements and around $50 an hour for preparing tax returns. If you are thinking the

national accounting firms are charging your company $75 an hour for staff accountants to do audit and tax work and $125 an hour for a partner's time, you are probably right, but it is not relevant to what you will be doing. You might even be making $50,000 or $100,000 a year as a corporate financial executive or corporate manager, but you still have to look at what the market will pay for the services you are planning on providing, not where you are coming from.

One of the first steps in developing our business plan will be to identify the specific target market we plan to market our services to. As you identify your potential market, find out what other competing services are charging in your local area. If you need to invoice $50 an hour to support your expenses and competitive rates are in the $35-$40 range your home-based business is already in trouble.

As an additional thought, do not think in terms of discounting your billing rates to reflect the savings you have as a home-based business. You should compete on quality of work with a comparable small office-based competitor. If you are going to give the financial benefits of having an office in your home to your clients you might as well have a normal office environment.

Another concern with discounting your services is the customer perception of value. If you are significantly less than competitive services or products the customer may perceive that your product is worth less. Through the home-based lease consulting and training business which I operate, my brother and I market PC based computer software which we developed. One of the systems which we developed, we advertised for $7,500 with the first users getting a test allowance of $3,000 for a net cost of $4,500. We felt this was reasonable, as we knew there would be bugs which we would have to fix and customer requirements which we had not originally thought of which would require modifications. Competitive products were selling between $10,000 and $15,000 so we thought we offered a very competitively priced product.

We generated a lot of leads from our advertising, but were surprised to find the leads were extremely difficult to convert to sales. As we sold our first few copies, however, and began to know the customers, several mentioned that during their evaluation process they were very impressed with the software design and functions which we offered in our product. Their initial hesitancy, however, was the price. It was too low! How could we develop a better software program than the rest of the industry and market it for half the price? The reality was that specialty software was very profitable. The materials cost for a computer program is nominal and the only real cost is overhead and the development time. As a small business, overhead was nominal and the development was done by myself and my brother.

This particular program took us a year to develop, test, and document; but it was mostly done during the evening and on weekends. I was actively involved during the day developing and teaching leasing seminars across the country. My brother was working with me while also consulting in computer systems design for his previous employer. He had requested a leave of absence to develop the system, but his company convinced him to continue working with them based on working twenty hours a week. They paid him 50% of his current salary and benefits as a consultant. The cost of development for us, therefore, was hardly anything. By passing this savings to the customer, we hurt our sales as the potential customers did not take our software as seriously as our competitors. I am convinced we would have been more successful had we priced our software around $10,000-$12,000 which would have put us right in line with the competing products.

Getting back to our business analysis, let's assume you can bill 15 hours a week for financial statement preparation and average 10 hours a week of tax preparation and consulting. This equates to 25 hours a week of billable time or a 63% billable rate. If this seems low keep in mind that marketing time, professional association meetings, ongoing training, vacations, holidays, sick time and the normal requirements of running a business are not billable. Besides if we wanted to work ourselves to death, we might as well keep a normal job!!!!

Given the 10 hours of "writeup" work at $25 an hour and 15 hours of tax work at $50 an hour this equates to an average weekly gross income of $1,000 or $52,000 for the year. We have not even considered our expenses yet, but we automatically know if you have a lifestyle which needs a gross of $75,000 a year you can not do it with a small accounting/tax preparation business unless you have a significant amount of interest, dividend, or retirement income. Gee, this feels like the beginning of a business plan!

If you have scaled down your lifestyle in anticipation of semi-retirement or a home-based business and think you can cover your expenses with the above gross then we will continue to refine our financial analysis to ensure the cash flow after business expenses will cover our cash requirements. In our case, our sample family should be very comfortable with a home based accounting\tax preparation business.

If it seems like we are spending a lot of effort to ensure that our home-based business concept will pay our monthly bills, it is because I believe most home-based entrepreneurs "jump" into business without a clue as to whether the business will support their earning expectations and needs. As an example, in one of our **PROFILES IN INDEPENDENCE** the owner said, *"I just couldn't stand my job any longer. A balloon arrangement was delivered to my boss, I said to myself I can do that, and gave them two weeks notice!"*

As it turned out, she could and has developed a successful home-based business, but it is sure a risky way to start a business.

Substitute **PLANNING** for faith, courage and hard work.

Well, maybe we can not eliminate the hard work, but planning and analysis can certainly enhance our courage and increase our chance of success. Failure is all right, but I sure hate paying for it so I am going to do every thing I can to maximize my chance for success and reduce the risk of failure. Didn't someone say, "If you've never failed, you've never tried anything!"

PERSONAL FINANCIAL PLANNING STEPS

1. Develop a personal budget and plan to live within it.

2. Get your credit cards under control! Get them paid off and try to keep them paid off each month. An annual interest rate of approximately 20% is a little expensive.

3. Perform a reasonableness test to ensure your proposed home-based business will support your income requirements.

4. Save until you have a minimum of 6 months of living expenses in liquid investments (Money Market Accounts or Certificates of Deposit). As you contemplate a home-based business, six months is the bare minimum with a year being better. I know you are thinking the money is going to roll in but it doesn't work that way. Also, the older you are the longer it will take to find a job, so your cash reserve needs to be larger in case your home-based business is not successful.

5. Use any additional cash to pay off consumer loans (cars, furniture, appliances, vacations, etc).

6. Invest any balance. Personal investment strategies.... sounds like another book.

7. Exercise Self Control: These steps are just common sense, but if you are having trouble managing a personal check book and your credit cards are a disaster how are you going to manage a home-based business?

TRUISM #2: DEVELOP A PERSONAL BUDGET AND TRY TO LIVE WITHIN IT.

CREDIT
CARDS

CHAPTER 2

BUSINESS
FINANCIAL PLANNING

Now that you have your personal financial plans in order, and you are still ready to charge ahead with a home-based business (at least you are still reading the book), we can begin to develop our Business Plan. The objective is not to end up with a formal Business Plan which is set in stone and then placed on the shelf and forgotten.  The value is in going through the thought process of evaluating your home-based business to develop a better handle on the initial startup costs, ongoing expenses, required equipment, potential customer base and to provide a marketing direction.

> **TRUISM # 3: DEVELOP A BUSINESS PLAN.**

If you do decide to formalize your Business Plan, the process is easier than you might think because you have already done most of the work. While you have been contemplating and thinking about starting a home-based business you have been mentally developing a

Business Plan all along. To formalize your Business Plan, just commit your planning process to writing. Putting your thoughts and plans on paper will also force you to evaluate objectively the potential success of your business idea. For a Business Plan, think in terms of the following sections:

BUSINESS PLAN

1. What is the Product or Service?
2. What is the Potential Market?
3. Who are the Specific customers?
4. Who is the Competition?
5. What is your Marketing Plan?
6. What Equipment (capital) is required to start?
7. What Operating Expenses will you incur each month?
8. What Marketing Expenses will you incur each month?
9. What is the Projected Revenue (Less Cost of Goods Sold)?
10. What is your Financing Plan for the Initial Equipment?
11. Develop a Cash Flow Schedule: Do you have financial resources to support the growth of your business?

If you want to formalize your Business Plan, also add the following sections:

12. Key Management Qualifications (You)
13. Personal Financial Statement

One value of formalizing your Business Plan in a written document is to begin developing a business relationship with your local bank. We will be discussing how to finance your home-based business, and your local bank is normally your last resort. As a business, however, you need to think in terms of future requirements.

One of the first steps in developing a relationship is to get to know your bank. Up to now, you probably deposit your paycheck, have a credit card or two, or three, or four, and an occasional car loan. You have probably never met a loan officer. Call the bank and ask for a loan officer. Ask him or her to lunch and get to know them. Explain about your home-based business, give them a copy of your Business Plan, and tell them you do not want anything from them! When they look puzzled, explain that you have the initial startup financing, but that you would like to begin to develop a banking relationship for future financing needs. You would also like to know who to call if you have a problem with your business account.

TRUISM # 3: GET TO KNOW YOUR LOCAL BANKER.

You pay for lunch! Who knows, the banker might even be impressed with your Business Plan. Solicit his advice. Ask if he has any suggestions or questions which you have not thought of. Get him on your team. You might never need a loan, but it is a small investment in the future. I work with a local bank in this fashion and even send the bank periodic financial statements. So far, I have only had one loan with them and it was a six month note. At the end of the six months, I paid off the loan even though the loan officer wanted to extend it. (They just love to collect that interest.) It is good to let the bank know you do not always need their money. It was nice, however, when I originally got the loan (which was unsecured) to just call up "my" banker, tell him how much I needed and go in and sign the paperwork. Although it was a personal loan for $15,000 the approval process was nominal, since I had been cultivating the bank relationship for two years.

It might seem like a trivial thought and not worth bothering with, but I almost never use the drive in teller. The local bank which I use is all on one level and the bank officers have offices opening into the main bank lobby. I usually make it a point to use the lobby teller and I always wave to the bank officers. If their doors are open, I occasionally stop by just to say hello. I only stay a few minutes, but I want them to see how often I am in their bank. I have several small home-based businesses and I am in the bank at least once or twice a week to deposit checks (OK! Once in a while to make a withdrawal). Everyone in that bank knows me.

If you are new to the bank, a Business Plan is the first step in this relationship. Unless you are looking for startup bank financing or an SBA (Small Business Administration) loan guarantee, do not pay to have someone develop the Business Plan for you. It should be your document, your roadmap to developing your home-based business.

As an additional thought, although you will read in a lot of business books about the advantages of being incorporated, when you meet with your local banker forget about the no-personal liability part. The lack of personal liability is great in a corporation to the degree it provides limited protection in a lawsuit, but it does not apply to your bank relationship. As a small home-based business, if you go into the bank asking for an unsecured loan with no personal liability you will get exactly what you are offering the bank. Nothing!

At best, you can hope for an unsecured line of credit based on your personal net worth and personal guarantee. More than likely, however, unless you have a pretty substantial net worth, expect the bank to offer a line of credit secured by your home equity, a certificate of deposit, or stock holdings. They will also insist upon a signature (personal guarantee) from your spouse. If all this seems unreasonable think about the recent Savings and Loan disaster and all the borrowers (including S&L officers and directors) who did not bother to pay back their loans. Many economists predict the same fate awaits the commercial bank system.

BUSINESS BUDGET

Now that your banker is impressed and we have planted a few seeds for future growth, we are ready to start on our Business Plan. The first step is to develop a budget of our fixed expenses. Later, as we further identify our marketing plans, we can budget additional costs (variable) such as advertising and marketing expenses which we have more control over.

Naturally, the total level of expenses will be different for each type of business, but in most home-based businesses the fixed costs of operating the business are about the same.

When we finish with the operating expenses, a later step will

be to develop an estimate of the capital investment required for startup equipment. This does not always have to be cash because many manufacturers or distributors offer financing incentives. Make sure you ask. They may offer leasing, rental programs, or even interest free financing for three months, or six months, or a year. If they do offer financing, which we feel is attractive, we will build the monthly cost into our operating budget. If not, we will have to figure out how to finance the equipment in the next section. In any event, just remember the old saying, *"You don't get what you don't ask for!"*

MONTHLY FIXED EXPENSES

	SAMPLE	YOURS
Rent	$ 0	
Electric	0	
Sewer, Water, Garbage	0	
Phone	50	
Office supplies	50	
Total	$ 100	

I knew there was a reason we liked home-based offices. In reviewing the fixed costs, we already have a home so the costs of our living environment should not change. There might be a slight increase in electricity if you are operating a lot of computer equipment, or in air conditioning since you will be home during the day, but I think the additional cost is nominal. A larger expense will be the increase in the cost of ice cream which you keep in the refrigerator. Well, you have to do something on your coffee break since you can not go down the hall and pester one of your office buddies.

TELEPHONE COSTS might seem a little high, but one of the things I highly recommend is to have a separate business line into your home. In the interviews for the book, a number of the home-based businesses operated with just their residential phone line, but the benefits of a business line far outweigh the additional cost.

The first benefit is simply to answer the phone with your business name. You could answer your residential line with your business name, but your friends might think you were a little strange. If you are reading this book and work for the local telephone company, you are probably thinking it is against the company rules to operate a business using a residential line. You are absolutely right, but this book is based on reality, or at least my perception of reality.

The second benefit of a separate business line is a listing in the telephone book under your company name. If a client can not recall your telephone number and they call information or look you up in the telephone book, guess what they will find if you are using your residential number? You are right. Nothing!

In addition to always answering the "business" telephone with your company name, keep the kids off the business line. In fact, do not even let them touch it, much less answer it. You will work hard as a home-based business to develop and maintain a professional image. The last thing you need is to have your seven year old answering the telephone! *"Yes, my daddy is here. What do you want him for?"*

Another recommendation is call waiting and call forwarding if they are available in your area. It is frustrating to call a business number and continually get a busy signal. At least with call waiting you can excuse yourself from the conversation, answer the telephone call and ask them to hold or offer to call them right back. Your home-based business and your livelihood are based on the calls you generate from your clients and customers. Call forwarding can be used to forward your calls to an answering service or to a mobile telephone which you can take with you if you are out of the "office" running errands.

The mobile telephone, by the way, is one of the world's greatest inventions. You can be anywhere. Your customer has no clue that while he is at the office in a suit and tie calling your office number, you are in the car on the way to Disney World or are already on the beach with a drink in one hand and his corporate proposal in the other. The reality is that a mobile telephone takes the place of a receptionist and at a much lower cost. I have recently seen mobile telephones advertised for $199 and the technology keeps getting more inexpensive. Mobile communications will eventually be like the razor blade and the razor. The telephone will become a commodity item with the money being made in providing the air time. Air time, by the way, is billed by the minute and is still pretty expensive, so keep in mind that the telephone is for business and not to call every relative you have, just to let them know you have a mobile telephone. You also pay for calls to your number as well as calls you place so do not give your mobile number to every friend that you have.

If you think I am exaggerating, just wait until you get the first bill from your mobile telephone company. It will show how many minutes of air time you are being billed for. You will absolutely swear that you did not talk that long. The introduction already explained about self-discipline so if you need to read that section again go ahead and turn back.

While we are talking about the telephone bill, another recommendation is an answering machine or a "voice mail" service. I do not particularly recommend a traditional answering service. Voice mail is probably my first recommendation as it is very professional sounding, is available twenty-four hours a day and is very reasonable. (Probably under $10 a month.) Most large corporations have installed a corporate voice mail system if their employees are unavailable, so it has become very common and accepted in the business community. Voice Mail is also available for personal computers, but unless you are a serious computer enthusiast, I would not recommend it. An answering machine is the second best alternative as it is essentially the same as a voice mail service.

The answering machine which I use has two prerecorded messages available, remote playback of the messages, and can even be turned on from a remote phone if I forget to turn it on. In actual practice, I have it set to answer on the fourth ring and I always leave it on. If I can not answer it by the fourth ring, then I figure I am unavailable. When I am around the house or running short errands (unless I have activated call forwarding), I use the first message which essentially says "*I'm in the office, but tied up on the computer and will return your call shortly.*" If I am out of the office for the day and do not want to be reached, I use the second message which essentially says, "*I'm in town this week, but out of the office on business and will return my calls tomorrow.*" If I am out of town traveling, then I change the message to indicate that, "*I am out of state teaching a seminar, but will call in for messages, and get back to them as soon as possible.*" The recorder even records the date and time each message is received, has a blinking light to let me know that I have messages, and says "good morning" when I enter the office. It's amazing what technology can do for a small home-based office. All right, it doesn't actually say "good morning", but I know it is thinking it.

In the interviews for the book, I was surprised with the range of telephone alternatives. A few of the businesses interviewed have exactly what I just recommended. Almost everyone had a basic answering machine and only one home-based business used an answering service. Voice mail through our local telephone company is not available in our exchange area yet and no one had a personal computer based voice mail system. One business with international orders communicated almost entirely with his fax machine due to the time difference between the United States and the far east.

The one business which uses an answering service was pleased with the service and felt the intangible value of having a person answer the phone was worth the additional cost. Based on other conversations with friends and small businessmen, however, the consistency and quality of service varies considerably from one answering service to another. In selecting an answering service, one of the things this Profile did was look for a small answering service which he felt could provide a more personal level of service. The particular answering service he selected also provides secretarial services and only has two answering service operators. He has also taken the time to ensure the answering service understands his business and knows where he generally is and if he is out of town when he will be back and how he can be reached. The extra time on his part in keeping the answering service informed and involved in his business has resulted in a more than satisfactory working relationship with his answering service.

If you should decide on an answering service the cost should be in the range of $50.00 to $100.00 a month. You may also want an answering machine as a backup in case you get calls from different time zones or evening calls from customers who know you work out of your home. You may not want to answer their call but you do want them to leave a message.

OFFICE SUPPLIES are also nominal as we are mostly talking about pencils, paper clips, note paper, stationary, envelopes, stamps, computer paper, etc. Most of these expenses are small and last a long time in a home-based office. I have excluded from this estimate postage and stationary used in a marketing program as we will cover the estimated cost and effectiveness of various direct mail programs in the chapter dealing with marketing.

MISCELLANEOUS expenses are incurred based on the type of business you are planning. To complete your budget of overhead or the costs of operating the office, estimate any miscellaneous costs which would apply to your business.

OFFICE EQUIPMENT

Office equipment is also dependent on the type of business you have in mind. As we discuss various types of equipment, if it does not apply to your proposed business then put the thoughts in the back of your mind for future reference.

TYPEWRITER: If your printing needs are extremely limited, then an inexpensive typewriter may be your best bet. By limited, I mean an occasional letter, invoice, and a few envelopes. If you have anything more than this, I would highly recommend a computer system unless you are a firm believer in opening a business on a shoe string and funds are extremely limited.

In 1984, when I first started my corporate training and software development company, letter quality printers were very expensive for personal computers, so for our correspondence and course manuals, I purchased a Canon AP350 Electronic Typewriter. At the time it was state of the art, stored page formats, had a text memory of 2,000 characters and displayed the last fifteen characters entered. I still have that typewriter and it is only used for an occasional envelope or a preprinted form. With the growth and availability of personal computers and their cost, I would really recommend a PC if at all possible.

Since we will be talking about how to finance the equipment for our home-based business, I should mention that a lot of companies have a demonstration program available, if you ask for it. When I first acquired the Canon Electronic Typewriter, I had just left

GTE and had scheduled and begun to advertise a public seminar on Computer Lease Negotiations for corporate personnel involved in acquiring computer equipment or working for a leasing company. In the meantime, I still had to write and type the course manual.

I went down to a local equipment dealer, found the electronic typewriter which I liked the best and asked if they had a demo program available so I could see if I liked it. The salesman told me to take it back to the office, try it for a week, and give him a call back. I took it home, spent day and night typing the course manual for the seminar and was finished by the end of the week. As it turned out, I liked the typewriter. We negotiated a purchase price and you already know what the next question was. *"What kind of financing program do you have available?"* The salesman offered bank financing at an interest rate which I can not recall. He settled on a small down payment and the balance in three equal monthly payments. I taught the seminar and used the money from the seminar to pay for the typewriter. I did not have to use any of my savings; the typewriter came out of funds generated by the business.

What's the moral of the story? First, ask for a trial demo period as you might not like the equipment. Second, if you do like the equipment negotiate a purchase price as if you were going to pay cash. Third, negotiate for payment terms with no interest. Fourth, do not buy a typewriter unless you absolutely can not afford or can not justify the cost of a computer system.

Remember, the price you get quoted for equipment is not the actual sales price of the equipment, it is just the starting point for negotiations. At the very least, ask if it is going to be on sale soon.

PERSONAL COMPUTERS:

In the next chapter on Marketing, we will be discussing the concept of personal marketing through speaking and publishing efforts to enhance our professional image and reputation. From a technical standpoint, a home-based office can prepare professional quality camera-ready copy for publishing pamphlets, books, marketing literature for mailings, and can prepare color slides and even color transparencies for overhead projectors. (OK! Color takes a little help from an outside source.)

From a cost and administrative standpoint, a home-based office can acquire office equipment at a price which just a few years back would have been prohibitive. Beginning with a personal computer as the backbone for your office we can build software and other office equipment around it.

In a generalized book, it is very difficult to encompass a wide audience with different financial situations, but in the case of a personal computer, I would suggest stretching the budget if possible. Even though an XT(8088 chip), or AT(286 chip) might satisfy your current office needs, a 386 based 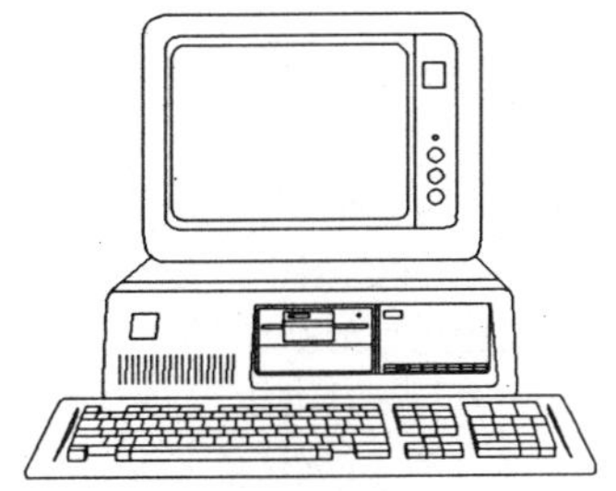 PC should meet your office computing requirements for the next three to five years. Based on a 386 (even a 386SX is acceptable) with some memory (preferably 2 to 4 megabytes of RAM) and a large hard drive (100 to 120 meg), we are in a position to run state of the art word processing software, a graphics program, a data base program, an accounting program, telecommunications through a modem, and maybe have enough memory left for a game or two.

From a cost standpoint, you should be able to purchase a 386 running at 33 Megahertz for under $2,000 including 4 megabytes of RAM, a 120 meg hard drive, both a 5 and 1/4 inch floppy disk drive and 3 and 1/2 inch disk drive, and an Enhanced VGA Color Monitor. As you lower your expectations or speed to 25 Megahertz, get lower resolution in a color monitor, or less memory in the hard disk drive the cost drops even more. A 386SX operating at 16 megahertz with a color VGA monitor, 40 meg hard drive, both floppy disk drives, and DOS should be in the range of $1,000. These numbers should provide a pretty good feel for the range of current pricing for IBM compatible personal computers. If you want more current pricing purchase a copy of any personal computer magazine such as *PC World, PC Magazine*, or an issue of *PC Sources* which is primarily a catalog of mail order computers, accessories, and software. If cost is a significant concern purchase on the bottom end, but if at all possible, try to stay in the 386 or 386SX line. You should be able to purchase a well equipped 386 at or below the costs quoted above. Given the cost decreases in computer equipment, by the time you read this book they will probably be even lower.

If you will notice the discussion so far has been based on an IBM compatible computer as opposed to Apple Corporation. I have to admit, I do not know much about Apple as an alternative personal computer. My perception is that Apple has built its' reputation primarily in the area of desktop publishing and ease of use through its' graphical operating system. Through a graphical interface the user controls the system by selecting or pointing (clicking a mouse) at pictures instead of memorizing and typing in operating commands. For example, to save a file the user points at a little file folder or to delete a file the user "clicks" on a picture of a garbage can.

Until the introduction of Microsoft Windows, the IBM compatible world has built its' customer following based on the extensive availability of business applications. Windows is just in the process of moving the IBM compatible or DOS (Disk Operating System) world into a graphical environment. I was just reading a computer magazine which estimated only 10% of IBM compatible personal computers installed are currently using Windows. I think the transition will occur, but over time, as users slowly move to Windows based applications. The point of all this, is that I have primarily used personal computers for business applications such as accounting and financial spreadsheets. Therefore, I am most comfortable with the world of IBM compatible computers. As a result, the hardware which I have mentioned and the software applications which we will be discussing are based on IBM or DOS compatibility and not Apple.

PRINTERS:

Once you have the base computing power, a printer and software are next. Keep in mind, we are discussing an office in which printed material is extremely important in enhancing our professional image. So if you are already thinking you can not afford it, think in terms of what it will cost to have marketing literature and brochures typeset and printed at the local printers. Printing, by the way, needs to be done on a laser printer printing at 300 DPI (dots per inch) as a minimum resolution. As an upgrade, however, Hewlett Packard markets a HP LaserJet III and associated models (IIIP for personal use) which utilize a Resolution Enhancement Technology to give the print resolution an even better appearance. While still printing at 300 DPI, the Resolution Enhancement Technology uses different size dots to smooth out the curves in the letters. The appearance of the enhanced printing looks better than standard 300 DPI but not as good as output printed at 600 DPI which we compared it to.

To give you a feel for the application of desktop publishing, print resolution of 600 DPI is a substantial improvement over 300

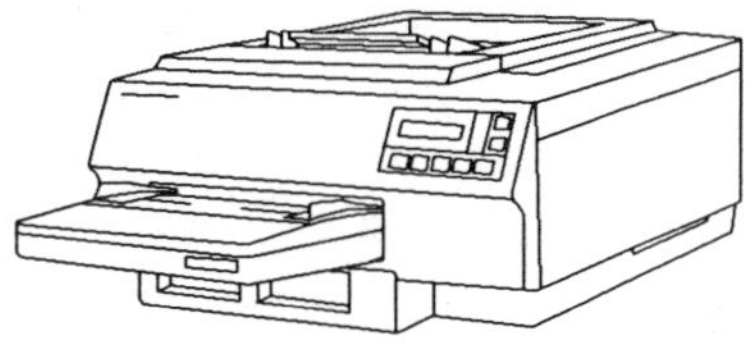

DPI and in my mind provides a master which is suitable as camera ready copy for the printing of any brochure, newsletter, pamphlet, or book which you might consider. Since laser technology was introduced, 300 DPI resolution has been accepted as the standard for business correspondence. The only thing holding back desktop publishing was the expense of increasing print resolution available to typeset quality which is in the area of 1200 DPI. The increase to 600 DPI, which is available from several companies, or an increase in appearance through a number of resolution enhancement techniques opens the door to professional quality publications prepared at home. The jump from 300 DPI to an appearance of 600 DPI is significant, while the jump from 600 DPI to 1200 DPI takes a magnifying glass or better eyes than mine to tell the difference.

This book, for example, was completely prepared except for the cover, using WordPerfect 5.1 to do all the word processing. All the graphics used for illustrations and to have some fun, were pulled directly into WordPerfect or edited through Harvard Graphics 3.0 and then imported into WordPerfect. The graphics were all commercially available software with most of the pictures from a company called New Vision Technologies, Inc., who developed and sells a graphics package called Presentation Task Force which can be purchased for less than $200.00. The final camera ready proof of the book was printed using a Hewlett Packard Laser Jet III and sent to a printer for publication.

A Laser Jet IIIP, by the way, can currently be purchased on a mail order basis for about $1,000. By the time you read this, it will probably be available for less. I was also just reading an advertisement by Lexmark, a subsidiary of IBM Corporation which now manufacturers and distributes IBM printers, announcing a new line of IBM LaserPrinters beginning with a Model 5E, 6, 10, and 10L. The entire Laserprinter line is 300 DPI resolution but utilizes a (PQET) Print Quality Enhancement Technology which the advertisement compares to the Hewlett Packard (RET) Resolution Enhancement Technology. Enhanced resolution appears to be the coming standard for laser printing. An interesting part of the advertisement, however, was the availability of a 600 DPI option using Adobe PostScript fonts. The 600 DPI option has a list price of $495 and also requires an additional four megabytes of printer memory (IBM list $799). As these printers become available in retail stores or through mail order, the price for the additional memory and the 600 DPI option will begin to drop.

The point is, once you eliminate commercial charges for typesetting and formatting a publication with different layouts, graphics, and font selections, the cost of preparing marketing brochures, articles, or flyers is significantly reduced. The cost is reduced to the point where there is no reason your marketing literature should not appear professionally prepared. If you are still thinking, *"I can't type and I don't want to learn to use all the software,"* just find a local home-based desktop publishing business. You will be amazed how cost effective their services are and the quality of the output. Of course, you will know what questions to ask, including what equipment they use. If you hear the word "laser" and the owner mentions 600 DPI or resolution enhancement instead of 300 DPI you have found the right place. Once you have prepared the camera-ready copy you will find the actual printing costs are very reasonable.

In this section on printers, I have used Hewlett Packard as the primary example because they seem to be the standard bearer for laser quality personal printers. There are also excellent models from other competitors that usually sell for a little less. As you assess your own need, this book is not intended to be a computer and printer shopping guide so you will have to decide which specific equipment to buy on your own. I will say, however, that I have used a Hewlett Packard LaserJet Series II printer for the last three or four years and it has never seen a service person. It is easy to add toner cartridges and I even upgraded the memory by myself. When I replace this model it will probably be with a Hewlett Packard LaserJet III and hopefully a 600 DPI upgrade.

From a cost standpoint you should be able to purchase a basic laser printer beginning around $600-$700. Although not an IBM or Hewlett Packard, a number of manufacturers market laser printers in this price range. If your business can not justify the use of a laser printer, then a dot matrix printer is probably your best option. Dot matrix printers can be purchased for less than $300 and provide excellent value for your internal printing requirements. I used an Okidata dot matrix printer for years and I am convinced that it is indestructible. I sold the Okidata to a friend who wanted to use tractor fed forms and it is still being used.

SLIDES AND OVERHEADS:

For oral presentations or seminars, overhead transparencies can be printed in black and white using almost any laser printer. Just run the overhead through the printer as if it were a sheet of paper. Insert it manually if your printer has any problem with the paper feed. Color presentations are almost as easy. Use your software to prepare the slide as you want the finished product to appear. Once you finish and save the file, the file can be transmitted by a modem or mailed on a diskette to any number of graphics slide services which support most personal computer based graphics programs. Harvard Graphics 3.0 even comes with a software driver and instructions to send color output through a modem to a company called Autographix, Inc. who offers overnight delivery of 35mm slides or overhead transparencies. There are also local graphics companies which will prepare slides for a cost ranging between $5.00 and $8.00 per slide.

SOFTWARE:

From a software standpoint, you need to assess your business requirements based on the type of product or service you are offering. If your computing and file keeping requirements are simple, an integrated package such as Microsoft Works or Lotus Works might serve your needs.

Integrated software contains a basic word processing system, data base manager for storing customer files, spreadsheet for financial calculations, and a communications module. Integrated software is often packaged as a starter system with the computer system which you purchase. If not included with your computer, Microsoft Works or Lotus Works can be purchased on a mail order basis for about $100.00 each. I mention mail order prices because there is usually a significant difference between mail order, discount, and list prices for software. Mail order is the least expensive, with discount software dealers next and retail software prices the highest.

For software, I do not have any hesitancy in recommending mail order services. The old argument retail computer stores used about providing software support does not seem to hold up too well as most software companies offer their own technical support for user questions and often include a toll free 1-800 number along with their software. In addition, I must admit, I can not recall the last time a retail computer store offered much software support.

To give you an example of the savings, I have been shopping for DrawPerfect which is a companion drawing and graphics program for WordPerfect. The best mail order price I have been able to find is $259 and the normal discount price from a software retail store who advertises discount prices is $349. This specific retail store just sent out a sales pamphlet which offered DrawPerfect for a special price of $299. I think the retail list price from the manufacturer is about $495, but as you can see the selling price is substantially different. Even the discount sales price was not as low as mail order.

Two cautions, however, if you order through the mail. Make sure the version number of the software is the latest available and use a credit card for the purchase. The credit card provides some protection should you not receive the software. Call the credit card company and state that you did not receive the product. Under the Fair Credit Billing Act you can claim a refund for goods and services not delivered.

WORD PROCESSING:

If you want more features and software support to generate different type styles (fonts) for your advertising and marketing then you should consider an upgraded word processing system. The three best sellers in the market are: 1. WordPerfect by WordPerfect Corporation 2. Word by Microsoft Corporation and 3. AmiPro by Lotus Development. According to computer literature, Word Perfect 5.1 and Microsoft Word 5.5 account for about 85% of IBM compatible word processing software sales to businesses and corporations.

WordPerfect is by far the more popular of the two. Version 5.1 is currently DOS based, but WordPerfect Corporation has just introduced WordPerfect for Windows. The Windows version will provide a screen which will appear exactly as the page will print WYSIWYG (What You See Is What You Get). I currently use Word Perfect and am completely sold on it. Microsoft Word also has two versions, Word and Word For Windows. Lotus AmiPro is also a Windows based word processing system. From a cost standpoint, they are about the same price with the Windows versions in the $300 mail order range and the DOS character based versions in the $250 range. If you plan to do much in the way of professional quality brochures, flyers, or marketing literature, I would suggest upgrading from a basic word processing software program to one of these three programs as a minimum.

Inexpensive desktop publishing programs are also available in the neighborhood of $100.00 each but I have found word processing software has satisfied my writing and marketing needs. Having said that, this book and most of my typing is done in WordPerfect 5.1, and I recently installed AmiPro by Lotus Development. I primarily installed AmiPro as a learning tool and an introduction to Windows based word processing. I have to admit, though, I am pretty impressed with the ease of use and value in having the screen look exactly as the page will print. It is also nice to resize and move graphics around the page by using the mouse. If I were just starting out with a home-based business and could afford the investment, I would recommend a Windows based word processor. Whether you choose Word For Windows, AmiPro, or WordPerfect For Windows is up to you. They will all satisfy your needs.

GRAPHICS SOFTWARE:

Depending on the amount you plan to write in terms of flyers, overheads, charts, and slide presentations that utilize graphics you might also think in terms of a graphics program. In the preparation of this book, a number of the graphics were imported from art files which I purchased. If you also noticed, a few have been edited to include word overlays to tailor the graphics to the book. This editing was done using Harvard Graphics 3.0, a graphics program by Software Publishing Corporation.

Harvard Graphics 3.0 (a recent upgrade from HG version 2.3), is primarily a business presentation program used to prepare financial graphs and presentations. I have also found it to be extremely useful in preparing advertising, graphics, and customizing drawings. Even the front cover, spine, and back cover of this book were prepared using HG3. The files were simply transferred and printed on a color printer and then given to the book printer as camera-ready copy.

As a result of the interviews and writing of this book, I plan to conduct a one-day public seminar on Starting A Home-Based Business. Who knows if the seminar will be successful, but the point is, the following advertisement announcing the seminar was prepared using HG3 and submitted as camera-ready copy to the local paper. It was prepared and printed on a Hewlett Packard LaserJet Series II in my home-based office. There are also other Graphics programs which compete with Harvard Graphics, such as DrawPerfect and Freelance Graphics 4.0 by Lotus Development. The graphics programs are in the $325 to $400 mail order range.

COMPETITIVE UPGRADES:

An option which you should also consider is competitive upgrades if still available through the manufacturers. For example, Lotus AmiPro is currently available for $99 if you own another word processing program which qualifies. Lotus also packaged Lotus 123 For Windows and AmiPro as an upgrade package for $149. When I purchased the AmiPro competitive upgrade, I did not really want Lotus 123 for Windows but for an additional $50 it seemed like too good a bargain to pass up. If any one has any Lotus 123 questions, give me a call as I am now learning how to use it. Freelance Graphics 4.0 was also available as a $99 competitive upgrade since I own Harvard Graphics. Word For Windows was available for $125 as a competitive upgrade. I told my wife I could not afford not to take advantage of all the savings.

She laughed, muttered something about a kid in a candy store and the Visa bill, and made me pick only one competitive upgrade. Since Lotus bundled AmiPro and Lotus 123 in one upgrade package, I figured that counted as only one purchase, so I bought it.

While editing this manuscript, WordPerfect also came out with a competitive upgrade program for DrawPerfect. As you know, I have been considering it as a companion program to WordPerfect 5.1.   Harvard Graphics 3.0 (HG3) is a great program, but the graphics transfer from HG3 to WordPerfect is a little awkward. The competitive upgrade price for DrawPerfect is $99. I will need to hide the American Express bill when it comes, but I will let you know how I like DrawPerfect.

FAX MACHINE:

Depending on the type of home-based business you are thinking about, you may also want to consider a fax machine if you send a lot of written proposals and need to communicate written information quickly to your clients.

Stand alone Fax Machines are available in most office supply discount stores for around $500. I have seen some as low as $400 and of course they also go much higher. You might also consider a fax board as an upgrade to your computers. Because I send very few faxes and receive even fewer, I installed a send/receive fax board which is also a 2400 Baud Modem in one of my computers. The cost was $150 but I have seen them advertised for a little less than that.

In hindsight, I have to admit that I should have purchased a stand alone Fax Machine. The draw back to the board is that the computer has to be on to receive a fax. If I am out of the office, I do not like to leave the computer running. If I am done working for the day, but am expecting a fax during the evening I still have to leave the computer on so the PC can receive the fax. I can only send faxes which I compose on the computer. If I want to send a preliminary contract or non-disclosure statement which a customer has mailed me to sign, I can not as they are preprinted forms.

With my fax board, I also need a separate phone line or a phone switch to differentiate between a personal phone call and a fax call. I have been trying to use my residential phone number as my fax number, so when a customer wants to send a fax I make it a point not to answer the phone. The particular fax board which I use can not tell the difference and tries to answer any call that comes in. If it is a fax call the board works fine. If it is a personal call the board tries to answer it also. A separate fax phone line would solve the problem, but that is another cost each month.

An electronic switch would also solve the problem but they are about $100. I could also have purchased a more expensive Fax Board. Had I known I would need a separate phone line or an electronic switch, I would have purchased a stand alone fax machine to start with. Since I get so few faxes, I have not purchased a switch yet and I am still using my residential line. If anyone wants to send a fax, I tell them to call me first and I will turn on the computer. I just have to remember that when the phone rings to let it continue ringing so the computer will pick up the fax message. I think I have it set to answer the fax on the fourth ring. It is a workable solution, but far from ideal.

CAPITAL BUDGET

Now that we have gotten a pretty good feel for the office equipment and software we are going to need, we are ready to begin developing a capital budget to start our home-based business.

Keep in mind that everyone has their own budget and willingness to invest in office equipment. In addition, each business is different with respect to the type of product or service they offer. Not all home-based businesses need the same amount of office equipment. The following table is my recommendation for a well equipped office assuming they send correspondence, write articles, and prepare advertising literature and are working with a limited budget. For the most part the prices represent mail order catalogs or discount office supply stores such as Pace Warehouse, WorkPlace, or OfficeDepot. I am sure you have similar outlet stores in your town or community.

Office furniture can encompass a wide range of furniture styles and quality from kits which you assemble to Ethan Allan. The dollar estimates provided are certainly modest and should cover basic furniture adequate for a home-based office. As you assess your own office requirements and personal preferences let your budget and Visa card limit be your guide.

INITIAL OFFICE EQUIPMENT

Office desk and chair	$ 200
3 Drawer Filing Cabinet	75
Bookcase	75
386SX/16 PC 1.2MB + 1.44MB floppy drives, 40MB hard drive, 14" VGA color monitor, 1Meg RAM, DOS 5.0, mouse	1,200
Okidata QL/00 Laser Printer	625
Phone with Answering Machine	75
WordPerfect 5.1	250
MoreFonts or Atech Publishers' Powerpack	60
Quicken (Accounting)	35
Total	$ 2,595

The above represents an estimate of a reasonably well equipped home-based office. WordPerfect with a Font (type styles) Program, will satisfy all your correspondence and marketing efforts. The Okidata Laser Printer, will produce excellent quality which you can use for your direct mailing and preparation of flyers.

Obviously, a home-based office can be started for less. In one interview, the only equipment the office has is a telephone. All the correspondence and consulting reports are prepared by a home-based secretarial service. This represents the extreme, but it works in this situation because Paul Walsh, working as a consultant, decided not to get involved in the computer equipment and word processing end of preparing his consulting reports.

If you have just a few more dollars available, about another $1,080 plus tax the following table shows an upgraded equipment base for the computer and laser printer. I know the personal computer configuration is available at the price shown because I am typing on it right now. It's nice! If the price seems low to you, reread the section about negotiations. If the price seems high, give me a call. I hate leaving money on the table. If you work for Okidata and you are thinking the Okidata QL400 is just as good as the Hewlett Packard IIIP, send me one to try out until the next revision to the book is available. In the interim, I have a bias towards HP because I have had such good service from my HP LaserJet Series II.

EQUIPMENT UPGRADE

386/33 PC 1.2MB +1.44MB floppy drives, 130MB IDE 17ms hard drive, 4MB RAM, 14" 1024 X 768 Super VGA Color Monitor, Mouse, DOS 5.0	$ 1,905 instead of $1,200
Hewlett Packard LaserJet IIIP Printer	1,000 instead of $625
Total Cost with Equipment Upgrades	$ 3,675

With the above equipment, you have an excellent base to grow with as you add future software or hardware upgrades.

OPERATING EQUIPMENT

As you assess your own home-based business, make a list of any required equipment you will need excluding the office equipment which we have identified to get us started. This list and the corresponding equipment cost will vary with each business.

OPERATING EQUIPMENT

FINANCING

Now that you have a total cost for the equipment which you are going to need, let us begin to talk about financing alternatives.

1. **CASH:** I know it hurts, but go ahead and write that check.

2. **CREDIT CARDS:** Credit cards should be a convenient way to acquire equipment, but only with the intent to pay off the cards (in full) when you get the billing. The drawback to credit cards is the high rate of interest which they charge. Most of the commercial credit cards which are available carry an interest rate APR (Annual Percentage Rate) anywhere from 15% to 22%.

This rate is even a little deceiving based on the way the different card companies compute interest. As you know, if you pay off the balance in full each month there is no interest charge. But what if you have a small balance such as $100 that you did not pay off? Three days before the end of the billing cycle for the current month you charge your $1,000 printer. How much interest do you owe? In all likelihood, the credit card company is going to charge based on the average balance using a simple monthly average instead of an average daily balance. In this case your average monthly balance was $600, the beginning balance plus the ending balance divided by two ($100 + $1,100)/2. If you are thinking you only had the use of the $1,000 for three days before the end of the billing cycle, you are correct. However, being correct does not save you any interest.

So now you have a credit card balance of $1,100 plus interest. The day you get the bill you send in a check for $750 thinking you will finish paying the balance next month. Assuming you did not buy anything else, your average balance is ($1,100 + $350)/2 so you are charged interest on $725 for a full month. I did not bother to add in interest for the prior month to make the example simple. The $350 ending balance was calculated by subtracting your $750 payment from your beginning balance of $1,100. If you are a banker reading this and you charge interest based on the average daily balance give me a call. If you are a banker reading this and "smiling," knowing how profitable credit card financing is, I hope you have a difficult time sleeping tonight!

The point is, credit card financing is very expensive and not a very economical way to finance long term equipment purchases.

3. **FINANCE COMPANIES**: When I purchased my latest PC, the dealer was more than willing to offer a 90 day or three month, no interest period. I am sure your dealer will be willing to do the same. The reason they are so accommodating is that a finance company is underwriting the cost.

Let me explain how this works. In order to qualify for the 90 days of free financing you have to fill out a credit application, qualify, and sign a consumer loan agreement with a credit company or bank. In all likelihood, the agreement will call for a minimum monthly payment and if the balance is not paid in full within the 90 days, the loan agreement automatically kicks in and you have a 24 or 36 month finance contract with equal monthly payments.

The reason the finance company is willing to underwrite the interest cost for three months is because they are charging at least 18% or more on the basic note and they are hoping you do not pay it off during the ninety day interest free period. Once you do convert to a consumer installment contract they probably have a prepayment penalty for early payment using a method called Rule Of 78's. Without getting into the way the payoff method works, just remember that the method benefits the finance company, not you.

Another little trick which I ran into recently was a service charge instead of an interest penalty for a late payment. We have a charge card for a local electronics and furniture store which advertises no interest on purchases paid within 90 days. If you do not payoff the purchase within the 90 days, the charge card is just like a credit card and is administered through a bank in Virginia. We made a purchase and about 45 days later received a late notice with a minimum payment of $13.00 due and a late payment penalty of $15.00. I have to admit, I hit the roof!! I called the bank, told them I had sent in payment in full and wanted to know how they could possibly charge a $15 interest penalty on a $13 minimum payment.

The bank said they had received my full payment and posted it the same day as the late payment notice was sent. They were sorry the late payment notice had been sent. Right! They then went on to say the $15 late payment charge was not an interest charge so usury laws did not apply (Somehow, I mentioned USURY in the conversation. I think I also mentioned something about thievery.) but the $15 was the minimum **SERVICE FEE** for a late payment. What a crock! Somehow I have a hard time distinguishing between an interest penalty and a service fee for a late payment, especially when the **service fee** is greater than the minimum payment.

4. BANK FINANCING:

Because we have taken the time to get to know our banker, financing for specific office equipment should be pretty easy to obtain. The interest rate should be substantially less than a Finance Company or your credit cards. I want to make a distinction here, between bank financing for office equipment and financing the start-up costs and operating expenses of a small home-based business.

Office equipment is usually easier to finance because the dollar value is not too large and the bank can see a tangible asset which you are acquiring. As a result they are more likely to make the loan. If you are asking for bank financing or a line of credit for working capital to cover operating expenses such as advertising, utilities, and salaries while you build your business, the bank will probably say no. I think the bank's basic feeling is that if you do not have enough capital investment to cover operating expenses, then the chance of your business succeeding is pretty low.

Office equipment loans, however, while primarily being evaluated as consumer credit based on your personal credit rating, at least offer the bank tangible security which they can place a lien against. The last thing the bank wants to do is sue for performance on the loan, or repossess the equipment, but, they do have that option.   If your home-based business requires special purpose equipment which has limited remarketability or the cost of equipment begins to increase, then you are stepping out of the world of consumer credit and into the world of commercial lending.

Commercial lending gets considerably more involved as the risk of loss and regulatory guidelines increase. Banks have to comply with Federal Deposit Insurance Corporation (FDIC) guidelines and audits if State Chartered or Office Of The Comptroller Of The Currency if Federally Chartered. Banks are also becoming concerned with Environmental Protection Agency (EPA) legislation with respect to property liability.   The particular bank I work with requires a Phase I Environmental Audit for any loan over $100,000 which includes real estate. To illustrate the concern with EPA liability, a friend is in the process of refinancing a 16 unit apartment building. The building originally had oil heating which my friend replaced with gas heating four or five years ago. The bank, with which he is refinancing wants the old, in-ground oil tank dug up and removed before they will close the loan.

The point is, as a small home-based business, if you want a short term loan to finance the purchase of office equipment, your bank is a viable source. If you are looking for working capital financing, a long term loan, or do not have an established credit rating, the bank is probably not an option.

5. **SECOND MORTGAGE:** One of the fastest growing methods of financing for the past few years has been a line of credit secured by a second mortgage on your personal residence. These loans have been very popular because the risk of default to the bank is very small. Of course, the contrast is that the risk to the borrower is substantial if you use the proceeds to finance a business and the business fails.

If you are determined to finance the acquisition of office equipment or specialized equipment for your business, however, then a line of credit is one of the most economical means. Due to the low rate of default, the interest rates are pretty low. The interest rate is usually adjustable and tied to the prime interest rate plus two or three percent.   In many cases, the bank or credit union will also pay the closing costs including an appraisal on your home, title insurance, and any taxes to set up the loan.

Take this word of caution, however, do not finance your operating costs for salaries and marketing with your line of credit. Also do not use your line for consumer purchases such as vacations, clothes, televisions, etc. The biggest problem with most lines of credit is that the borrowers slowly borrow against them because it is so easy to just write a check. Pretty soon, the line of credit is full and becomes another long term loan just like your first mortgage. Do you remember the earlier part of the book about exercising self control?

I have a partner in an apartment investment who formed a wholesale specialty food supply business a few years back. He financed most of the investment and his partner provided the expertise and managed the daily operations. When the business failed, his partner left town and has not been heard of since. In the meantime, my friend secured a second mortgage on his home to pay off the short term debts which he had incurred to start and operate the business. Failure can happen! Do not bet your future on the success of one business venture. Do you want to hear about the medical supply business I helped start? I knew it was over when a partner left a van full of medical supplies and medical kits in my driveway late one night. In fact, writing this book made me realize I have not heard from my partner since he left town either. Limit your downside risk!

As you use the line of credit, also try to match your repayment with the life of the asset. For example, if you finance a personal computer and estimate you will use the computer for three years then try to pay off the computer loan by making 36 equal monthly payments on your line of credit. The equal payments will make budgeting easier and have the loan paid off when you are ready to upgrade or replace the computer. As you purchase additional equipment, increase your loan payment based on the life of the new equipment. If you do not exercise this self discipline and make payments on your line of credit as you can, you will end up ready to buy new equipment and the old equipment will only be half paid off. It is the same concept as buying a car and financing it for ten years. You know you will not have it for ten years.

6. **LEASING**: For small dollar items leasing is best viewed simply as an additional source of financing. Traditionally, we think in terms of leasing equipment when we have a short term need for the equipment or where the lessor (the owner of the equipment) assumes the residual risk of remarketing the equipment when the lessee (user)

returns it. This is generally true, but it does not apply to what the industry calls "small ticket" or "money over money" lease transactions.

To define small ticket leases, we are primarily dealing with equipment costing less than $100,000. In this price range, the lease is really a secured loan in which the lessor, instead of the lessee, gets to keep the equipment at the end of the loan. If we solved for the interest rate on a typical $10,000 office equipment lease, the rate would probably be about the same as a credit card.

To make matters worse, once we have paid for the equipment through the lease, at the end we get to buy it again. In all likelihood, the lessor will probably end up selling you the equipment for 10%-20% of the original equipment cost at the end of the lease. The second area of concern is that the lease term is a non-cancelable term. In a credit union or bank loan, we can go in a pay off the remaining balance. A bank might charge us a small penalty by using the Rule of 78's, but at least we have the option to pay off the loan. In a lease, we do not even have the option. Would you like to pay off the lease? Certainly, just pay the remaining payments.

For large equipment purchases, in the millions of dollars, leasing may be economically attractive because leasing becomes an investment decision based on extensive financial and contractual negotiations. For small consumers, however, leasing is an emotional issue based on monthly cash flow or ease and convenience of financing and it will generally cost you more than conventional bank or credit union financing.

This may be opposite of what you understood and what equipment salespeople and car leasing companies have been telling you. To illustrate the point, the following example is based on a car lease. Car leasing is a little different due to the tax considerations if you use your car for business, but for now see if you can calculate the interest rate the lessor is charging the lessee in the following example.

LEASE EXAMPLE

A lessor has offered a lease rate of $245 per month for 60 months. Lease payments are due in advance on the first of each month. The list price of the car is $15,000 but as the buyer you know you can purchase the car for $13,500 if you pay cash or finance the purchase at the bank. In addition to the first lease payment, at the closing the lessor also charges a $200 non refundable application fee and a $300 security deposit which is refunded (no interest) at the end of the lease. At the end of the lease, the lessor has a Terminal Rental Adjustment Clause (TRAC lease also known as a open end lease) of $4,500. The lessee has the option to buy the car for the guaranteed purchase option (TRAC) of $4,500 or return the car. If the lessee returns the car and the lessor sells it for less than $4,500 the lessee has to make up the difference.

If the customer decides to purchase the car initially and finance it through a local bank the interest rate is 12% with 60 monthly payments of $300.30 based on financing $13,500.

Assuming you purchase the car at the end of the lease, see if you can figure out what interest rate the lessor is charging you? Does the example look confusing? It was meant to. The lessor does not want you to focus on all the mathematics. The lessor wants you to focus on the lease payment of $245 per month in comparison with the loan payment of $300.30 per month. Think how you can take the savings each month and invest it at 1,000% per year. Besides, by saving the difference each month, you can get a nicer car than you had originally planned on. You work hard, you deserve it. Your family deserves it.

While you are working on this problem, I want you to remember that I am writing this book for fun. For the last eight years, I have made my living teaching corporate leasing seminars that last from one to three days depending on the specific client. For lessees, I teach a Lease Negotiations Workshop. For lessors, I teach a Lease Marketing Skills Workshop.

To solve the problem, you need a calculator which will solve for present values such as a Hewlett Packard 12C, 10B, 17B, 19B or Texas Instruments BA35 (the TI Business Analyst II will not work), or a Sharp EL-733. The secret is to identify the cash flows and then solve for the interest rate.

Beginning Cash Flow	Ending Cash Flow
$13,500 Inflow	$4,500 Outflow
300 Outflow (Deposit)	<u>300</u> Inflow
<u>200</u> Outflow (Application Fee)	
$13,000 Net Cash Inflow	$4,200 Net Cash Outflow

Set your calculator to payments in advance:

$13,000	Present Value (PV)
- 245	Payment (PMT)
- 4,200	Future Value (FV) Final Cash Outflow
60	Number of Months (N)

i	Solve for interest rate (i)
X 12	Multiply by 12 to get an annual rate

i = 13.25 %   Leasing Company Interest Rate

In this case you are paying 12% interest at the bank while the leasing company is charging you an interest rate of 13.25%. I intentionally made the example come out reasonably close, but before you lease any equipment use the same technique to solve for the interest rate. As an initial calculation for an equipment lease which does not have a residual value guarantee use a residual or future value of zero. If the interest rate is greater than your borrowing rate at the bank, then do not lease (unless you need the equipment and the bank will not lend you any money).

When you are negotiating that lease or bank loan, even if you can not remember how to solve for the interest rate using the calculator, take it out of your pocket and set the calculator on the desk anyway. Don't even pick it up again. But as you are placing it on the desk say, *"Is that the best you can do?"*

7. **FRIENDS AND RELATIVES**: Now we are down to the best and worst sources of investment capital. Best, because our friends or relatives might be willing to loan us funds at a reasonable interest rate and without getting rug burns on our knees while begging in our banker's office. Worst, because if we do not pay them back you have lost a friend. It is difficult to lose a relative, although you might have a few you wish you could lose.

If you do not pay the loan back, you might have a relative who wished they had never known you. You have to make the decision. I have known relatives who were able to operate as partners in business ventures together and relatives who made loans to each other. In some cases it worked out and in others, the relatives are hardly speaking with each other. Just remember, relatives are family for life. If you are not absolutely committed to paying them back think in terms of a bank loan or second mortgage on your home.

With friends, it is a little different. Friends are in a better position to make a rational decision in evaluating a personal loan or potential investment if you are looking for a partner. As long as the friends recognize the risk in starting a home-based business and are willing to assume that risk, then an investment or loan is acceptable. I have investment partners who are friends and in some cases we have made money and in other cases we lost money. We all understand the risk.

Relatives, on the other hand, have a greater emotional involvement in wanting you to succeed and not wanting to create any family animosity by saying "No" when they do not want to make the loan. Relatives should be your last source of financing.

8. **VENDORS**: The equipment dealer or manufacturer is often the best source of financing because they have a vested interest in wanting you to purchase the equipment. Always ask if either the dealer or the manufacturer has a financing program available.

Just like automobile manufacturers, they might have a low interest rate program available. The dealer might be willing to accept equal payments over three months with no interest. The dealer might even be willing to finance the equipment over a longer term. Keep in mind the dealer may be a small business person like yourself and have limited ability to finance a sale. But on the other hand, if the equipment is in their showroom, the dealer is probably incurring an interest expense to finance their inventory plus they want to make a profit on the sale to you.

It does not seem unreasonable to negotiate financing terms as well as or instead of a discount on the purchase price. Certainly, you were not planning on paying the list price.

REVENUE AND PRICING

I have already mentioned the concept of pricing and the option of pricing based on an hourly rate or based on a product. Recognize that a product may also be a service. To expand this concept, let me say right up front, you will make more money if you price by the job as opposed to pricing by the hour.

To illustrate this concept, automotive repair work is a good example. If you take your car in for repair and ask what the hourly rate is, the service department will quote a rate. Assume the hourly rate is $30 an hour which seems reasonable to you. When they actually make the repair, however, most automotive dealerships or service companies do not charge by the actual time it takes to make the repair. Instead they charge based on a standard which has been developed for each job. Assume your repair had a book standard of three hours, but the repairman finishes the job in two hours and fifteen minutes. What do you get billed for?

You will usually get billed for three hours of labor at whatever the hourly rate is. Why do they operate in this manner? Two reasons, first of all, a standard number of hours for a given job makes it easy to provide a customer an estimate of their repair bill and, secondly, the repair people know they will make more money. They make more because they almost always beat the repair standard. The faster they get finished the more money they make. Most repairmen are paid a percentage of the labor cost for their work and are not paid by the hour.

Does this seem a little deceptive? It probably is if the customer is not aware of the practice. For example, I had some engine work done on one of my cars in which the dealer had to take off the air conditioning compressor. As he was putting the compressor back on he asked if I wanted him to put on a new air conditioner belt while he was at it? I said, "*Sure*," thinking I would save the future labor expense if a belt broke because there was no additional labor to put a new belt on instead of the old belt. When I got the bill, one of the itemized charges was $40 for replacing the air conditioning belt. I was confused and asked the service department about the charge. The service manager said the standard labor charge to change an air conditioning belt was 1 hour since the compressor had to be removed. I argued that the compressor was already off, all the repairman had to do was put back the new one instead of the old one. I still had to pay the $40 because they charge based on standard labor not on actual labor. Of course, they do not charge me anymore. I have not been back.

The point is, charging by the job is usually more profitable than charging for actual time. Based on this concept, check competitive charges and quotes based on the value of the job and not the actual time. Recognize, once in a while, you will make less, but the averages are in your favor. Just like the automotive repairman, if they take a car back because the customer was not satisfied the first time, the repairman has to correct the problem for free. Of course, in our case the service or product will be first class, but if you quote based on the job once in a while the customer will not be satisfied and you will need to make revisions or redo part of the job. Even if it is the customer's fault, view the time as an investment in customer service.

If you utilize computer equipment or expensive equipment, it is also difficult to bill based on time because how do you factor in the cost of the equipment? In my wife's accounting firm, tax preparation was all done by computer. The actual time to prepare a return consisted of the interview, putting the data in the computer, and reviewing the tax return for errors and potential areas to save the customer any taxes. Of course, there was a significant investment in computers, software, overhead for the office, and ongoing training to stay current with tax law changes. To address this problem, they developed a billing rate for each schedule on a tax return.

If a customer came in and requested an estimate, it was easy. The estimate was based on the number of schedules the customer required. As they were doing the work and the customer needed additional schedules because they forget to mention the out of state rental property which required an additional schedule on the federal return and filing a return in a different state, the additional charges were easy to identify and justify. They simply provided each customer with a price list identifying the charge per schedule.

Another drawback to charging by the hour is that most customers want an estimate and are not very understanding if the estimate is off. When Sandy first started the accounting firm, they charged by the hour. They might estimate that a return would take a couple of hours and provide the customer an $80 estimate. I was amazed how often she came home upset because a customer had given her a hard time because the final bill was $100 for two and a half hours instead of two hours. It did not matter that the customer brought their receipts in a paper bag or forgot to mention several schedules. All the customer remembered was that the estimate had been $80. Of course, no one complained if the actual time and billing turned out to be less.

Moving to the fixed charge per schedule solved a lot of their pricing problems. In another profile, as I was interviewing A-Team Cleaning Service, who provides commercial cleaning services, I asked how they estimated and billed each job. They bill based on a flat rate per month and the initial estimate is based on their estimate of the number of hours it will take, an estimate of cleaning materials, and a markup to cover their investment in cleaning equipment and a profit. When the contracts are renewed they compare their actual hours with their original estimate to see if they need to raise the monthly charge. With a fixed monthly contract the customers know exactly what their billing will be. I asked if they had a specific hourly rate which they tried to earn for themselves? I am sure Jan and Mary did, but they laughed and were not telling me.

In almost every profile, the businesses have billing rates for specific jobs or services, and did not bill by the hour. In my case, I have a seminar rate based on a one day, two day, or three day seminar. I do not have an hourly rate unless someone wants me to do a specific consulting assignment.

Globe-Con International charges a percentage markup based on the cost of the order. D & B Credit Consulting charges for their services based on a percentage of the past due accounts collected. D & B Credit Consulting also has an increasing percentage based on how long the account has been outstanding. The Flyer Service charges based on each flyer delivered. Accounting is probably one of the few areas where services are occasionally provided based on a hourly rate.

BUSINESS PLANNING

Hopefully, you have gotten a feel for the cost of acquiring and financing the equipment you will need in starting a home-based business. We have also started developing a business relationship with our bank, and you have given some thought to developing a billing or pricing schedule for the products or services you plan to offer. With this foundation, we are ready to begin developing a Marketing Plan as the next step in our overall Business Plan.

CHAPTER 3

MARKETING PLAN

It might seem strange to start a chapter on marketing this early in the book when we have not even gotten to business structures, or taxes, or basic accounting, or office management, or all the other good stuff which we need to know to start a business. It might be early in the book, but I assure you **MARKETING** is the most important aspect of your business. If you can not market your product or services

you do not need to know all the "other" stuff. You do not need to worry about office equipment or accounting because you will not have any revenue to account for.

Marketing is going to be your biggest challenge! In every interview which I conducted for this book, every entrepreneur said doing the work (whatever their product or service) was the easiest part of being in business for yourself. Not a single person questioned their ability to provide their service. They all were concerned with marketing and getting the work into the office. I would venture that you will spend at least 25% of your productive time marketing.

In the rest of the chapter, we are going to approach marketing from a number of perspectives based on the type of business you have identified. Once you have identified the type of business and product or service you plan to enter, the first thing you must do is ask yourself, "*Who am I going to sell to?*" From a textbook standpoint we are talking about market segmentation or identifying your specific target market.

IDENTIFY YOUR POTENTIAL CUSTOMER

Who Am I going to sell to? This sounds like a pretty basic question and it should be, but a small home-based business may not always adequately identify who they are trying to sell to. To put the question another way, "*Who is going to pay for what I have to offer?*" You might have the best idea in the world, but is there a foundation of long term customers willing to pay for the service?

Once you determine there is an economic base for your service, you need to identify the specific target market you want to market to. If you want to sell dental supplies, every dentist in the area is a potential customer. In one of the profiles, Don Pressler specifically defined his target market as wholesale petroleum equipment distributors and suppliers in the State of Florida. Representing five manufactures of petroleum equipment and supplies, Don calls on about two hundred companies who operate in the state selling petroleum equipment and supplies to gasoline stations, oil change services, and direct to large commercial users. If Don had defined his target market to include the retail petroleum sellers, instead of two hundred wholesale customers he would have 10,000 potential accounts.

Define a target market that you can effectively handle. In another profile, Brenda Saling provides dog obedience training services. Clearly, she has specifically identified existing or potential dog owners, but how do you effectively market to such a broad based and changing market?

Now that you have identified a target market, and in most cases, a home-based business will be providing services or products in the local community, how do we begin to market our services? Assuming you will be marketing in your local community, the first thing you do is tell everyone you know that you are going into business for yourself.

TRUISM # 5: TELL EVERYONE YOU KNOW THAT YOU'RE IN BUSINESS AND ASK FOR REFERRALS.

In every profile and interview, the number one source of business was personal referrals from friends or existing business contacts. You are probably thinking this is too simplistic again. Or, you might be thinking, "*I hate to impose on my friends by asking for referrals.*" Just to clear up this misconception, if they are your friends you are not imposing. To illustrate this, think in terms of yourself. When a friend asks you for a recommendation for a specific service such as an accountant, or lawyer, or carpenter, just who do you recommend? You recommend other friends who can provide the desired service or professionals who have earned your respect with the quality of professional service or products which they have provided to you.

In fact, when you are looking for a professional service asking your friends for referrals is the first thing you do. How could it possibly be an imposition on your friends to let them know you are in business for yourself and you would appreciate any referrals? The only time you are imposing is if you can not perform the service. That is a quandary. But, of course, that does not apply to our situation. Isn't there an old saying that we can paraphrase, "*The whole world is a little incompetent, except for you and I, and I'm not real sure about you?*"

The second source you ask for referrals is other professional contacts, so let all your business contacts also know that you are in business. You will be amazed at all the round about routes referrals get passed along and end up with you. From your friend, to his cousin, to his cousin's barber, to the barber's wife's bridge club, to the club manager who calls and says, "*A close friend recommended you and we were wondering if you could.................? Wholesale, of course?*"

Now that you have told everyone that you know, let us begin to get more specific with our marketing plans based on your assessment of who your potential customer is. The identification of your potential customer is critical, however, as your marketing plan will be based on the type of customer you have defined, the size of the potential market segment, and the best ways to establish personal credibility while marketing yourself and your services.

Essentially, we are going to divide marketing into two distinct approaches. One is **personal marketing** in which the target market

is a well defined population which we can identify and specifically market to. The second is **mass marketing** in which the whole world or at least our local community is a potential market. In each case a different marketing approach is required because in mass marketing we can not specifically identify who our customer will be. Instead of a specific customer we can call on or send a direct mailing to, we are dealing in a world of numbers and statistical probability. For example, in most direct mailing programs a customer response rate in the range of 1%-2% is expected. Direct mail, therefore, becomes a game of numbers. The more you send out, the better your response.

TRUISM # 6: GET INVOLVED IN YOUR COMMUNITY.

If you are going to be involved in your local community in a home-based business, you need to get to know the other businesses in your area. Not only can they provide a source of business to you, but you may need their services for your business. The best way to get to know your fellow businesses is to join and get involved in the local Chamber of Commerce.

The cost to join is normally pretty reasonable. The Chamber probably has a once a month luncheon meeting, new member receptions, and ongoing community programs. Our Chamber even has a Business After Hours Program which is a once a month reception sponsored by a new member at their office. The intent is to get to know the new members and as well as seeing their office location and getting a feel for their products or services.

As a home-based business, you probably do not want to sponsor a reception, but it would be a good opportunity to get to know the other members. Keep in mind, if no one knows you are in business, it is difficult to send referrals.

Our Chamber also sponsors a Leadership Program, which consists of ten weekly meetings with other participants invited to join the Leadership Program and learn about how the community functions. Community leaders are invited to speak at the meetings, as well as field trips to meet with county leadership and tour community services such as schools, hospitals, and the legal system. In addition to the leadership skills gained and a better understanding of how the community functions, the participants also develop a sense of fellowship and network of business associates which lasts a lifetime.

The second source of networking and community involvement, is to join a community civic association. The same concepts as the Chamber of Commerce apply, except the civic associations are smaller, you get to know the members better, and usually meet on a weekly basis. Which association you decide to join is certainly up to you. They are all good. I am more familiar with the Kiwanis, but ask a few of your friends, or attend some of the different meetings and join the association which you feel most comfortable with. One key, however, is that you need to get involved, not just join. If you join and do not attend the functions it is a waste of your money. If you accept a volunteer position and do not do the job, instead of gaining friends and potential business contacts you are building a negative reputation.

The third source of community and professional growth, is to join and get involved in your local professional association. For example, if you are an accountant get involved in the local chapter of your State Association of Certified Public Accountants or the State Association of Independent Accountants, if you are not certified. If you are a consultant in data processing get involved in the local chapter of the Data Processing Management Association (DPMA). If you teach seminars or speak professionally, join the local chapter of the National Speakers Association or the American Society of Trainers and Developers (ASTD). If you have a professional background, there is probably a professional association which you can join, get involved in, and hopefully get a few referrals from as you grow your new business.

If you are thinking this sounds like a lot of work and involvement, it is. You did not think success was going to come easy did you? If it did, we would all be successful, rich, and famous. I keep stressing that a home-based business is a business. Just because we are operating from our home does not change the basic aspects of conceptualizing, growing, and nurturing a business. Being at home only cuts down on our overhead and gives us a greater chance of being successful.

> **TRUISM # 7: THE MORE PERSONAL YOUR PRODUCT OR SERVICE IS PERCEIVED TO BE, THE MORE PERSONAL YOUR MARKETING HAS TO BE.**

PERSONAL MARKETING

Initially, let us start with a personal service which requires a high degree of professional competence and reputation and as a result has a limited market. Consulting engagements, conducting professional training seminars, accounting, or personal financial planning would be examples in which the entrepreneur must first establish professional expertise and credibility in the specific field.

The following list identifies specific marketing strategies which create or enhance a professional reputation and generate the most productive leads. Keep in mind these are based on my experiences and interviews conducted with successful home-based businesses. As I have stated before, if you disagree with the ranking or any of the individual suggestions just ignore them. That is part of the benefit of being your own boss. You only have to listen to ideas you agree with!

1. **PERSONAL REFERRALS**: I have already stated the best lead is a personal referral from a mutual acquaintance or someone you are currently doing work for. Did you think something else would be first on our list?

2. **SPEAKING ENGAGEMENTS**: Give speeches or conduct seminars on your specialty at Professional Trade Association Meetings or speak at Civic Association meetings in which the audience consists of potential clients.

Every public speaker in the world starts out on the "roast beef and mashed potatoes" circuit at local civic association meetings to begin developing name recognition and credibility. The same concept applies to professional trade association meetings. They all have monthly dinner meetings for which they are looking for professional speakers or ongoing continuing education meeting for which they must find qualified technical speakers or workshop leaders. Just call the trade association, ask for the Program Committee Chairman and give them a call. The Chairman will be delighted you called because finding speakers for each program is a time consuming and thankless volunteer job.

As a speaker, you will instantly gain recognition as an authority by virtue of being on the program.   Once you finish speaking, that engagement now becomes part of your professional credentials and literature and is noteworthy as a potential press release.   You will be surprised how often local newspapers will publish a news release which you have sent in.   Professional Associations also publish news releases pertaining to speaking engagements.

I belong to the Florida Institute of CPA's and every month the association magazine has a section on company announcements and presentations given by members of the association.   In our particular profession as public accountants, I believe the speaking announcements and occasional pictures are to positively show that accountants can speak in public, do not have green eye shades, and that someone does love us.

3. **MAGAZINE ARTICLES**: Submit professional articles for publication by trade association publications or specialty magazines on both a local, state, and national level. These are mostly unpaid, unfortunately, but they develop an amazing amount of professional credibility.

Also keep in mind that every local chapter newsletter is usually begging for articles. Even a chapter newsletter has value in your local community. While getting paid for the article would be great, your chances are not too good. The trade journals will, however, include a biographical sketch and often a photograph. You might even suggest a tradeout for advertising space. This is especially applicable if you are writing a specific article which the association or magazine has an interest in. To find out, just call the magazine editor, ask if they have a master schedule of topics for upcoming magazines, and are they looking for articles on any of the specific subjects? Most magazines do have specific topics scheduled for each month as they use this list to schedule inhouse articles, freelance writers, and in selling advertising space.

If you have contacted a magazine which appears to be related to your field but you are not familiar with the magazine, you might want to find out more about the demographics of the readers. If so, ask for a "Media Kit" which is available to potential advertisers and describes the circulation, income levels, and specific areas of interest.

As an additional thought, a magazine article is not intended to be a complete review of your specific expertise. It should be a teaser. An article should get the readers attention, hold their interest through the end of the article and always leave them wanting more! That is the key. You want to leave them hungry. You want to have them saying to themselves, *"This person can help my company."* With this in mind, write articles which deal with potential problems or "how to" type articles. For example, the first article I published in a national newsletter was entitled "TAX REFORM AND LEASING SPECIALIZATION." The article dealt with the potential impact of the Tax Reform Act of 1986 on the Equipment Leasing Industry. The specific content is not important, but it is an example of an article designed to entice a response from the reader. A response hopefully leading to consulting or training seminars with the reader.

If you are still unsure, start your article with "Six Sure Ways To Increase Inventory Turnover," or "Five Steps To Effective Marketing." It can even be an article for a small local publication. "Five Steps To Save Cleaning $$," or "Six Ideal Plants For Low Maintenance Landscaping." The point is, **How To** articles quickly get the readers attention, are easy to write, easy to get published, and establish your reputation as an authority in your specific field.

4. **NEWSPAPER ARTICLES**: The same concept of getting articles published in magazines applies to local newspapers. Usually every town has a metropolitan newspaper, but there are often local community newspapers which specialize in the community or suburb which you live or work in.

In fact, to compete with the local nature of many community daily or weekly papers, many municipal papers publish multiple editions with a local section which only contains articles of local interest. How do you think they get these articles? Why not submit a "How To" article yourself? While working on this book, one of the profiles called me and asked if I would mind if the community newspaper used some quotes from the Profile which I wrote? She went on to explain that she had shown her Profile to a friend, who worked for the community "weekly," and her friend wanted to do a local interest article. No! Not on my book, but on how she developed her home-based business.

Think of the potential benefit. Another Profile just showed me an article on personal growth which he submitted to our metropolitan newspaper. It was the first of a series of articles (hopefully an ongoing column) which he proposed writing for the newspaper. He does not care if he gets paid or not; the intent of the column or series of special interest articles (over and above personal satisfaction) is additional professional credibility and name recognition for a Personal Growth Workshop which he conducts.

If he gets published, think of the potential marketing exposure. What would it cost if he had to pay for fifteen or twenty column inches of advertising in the paper? In almost every business Profile in this book, the owner could write a local interest article which would have a good chance of getting published. They could write articles like "Tax Saving Tips," "The Importance of Using Sun Protection," "How To Blend Personal and Corporate Growth," "How To Verify Your Own Credit Record," or "Social Security And Retirement Planning."

The point is, if you have a home-based business you have a product or service to sell. Tell the public about the benefits of the product or if you are offering a service, tell the public how knowledge about what you know will directly help them. Write the article as an information service or based on a "How To" approach and you have got a good chance of getting it published.

5. **NEWSLETTERS AND PERSONAL CALLS**: A newsletter follows the concept of an article but you incur the cost of publishing it. Find a local home-based desk-top publisher and you will be surprised how inexpensive it is to produce an 11" by 17" single fold newsletter on a personal computer, print it on a laser printer and have one or two thousand copies produced at a local print shop.

Once you have identified your specific target market, follow up mailing the newsletter with a personal visit. I recognize we are limited by the geography of the target market, but if your customer base is in a local community you will get the most benefit from a person to person meeting. If your customer base is too large to visit personally, then follow up the mailing with a personal telephone call. Without the call or visit, the effectiveness of your newsletter is significantly reduced.

If you do not like "cold" calls, think of the alternative if you do not establish a customer base. The newsletter, however, can serve as an ice breaker. Have a copy in your hand and say, *"Hi, I'm Gene Pike, I'm a local accountant and I recently sent a newsletter on business tax tips which I thought you might find interesting. I've just opened my accounting firm and wanted to stop by to make sure you got a copy and to introduce myself.*"   From that opening, just let the conversation follow its' own course. The key point is that the call is not a hard sell. It is only an introduction and a follow up on the newsletter. Be friendly. Smile. Ask what his firm does if it is not apparent.

Give the business a contact or referral if you can. *"Gee, I just met so and so, who has opened up a new ....office. He's going to need a ...."* It is amazing the network that gets developed just by meeting all the new and established businesses which you have identified as your potential market.

If you will also notice, you are not pressing for any business so your marketing call is very low key. Set a goal. Follow up or call on 25 potential business contacts a week. Make yourself meet that goal. Pretty soon you will be saying, *"I can't, I'm too busy doing the work I have now."* Just keep in mind that if you wait in your office for business to come to you, you will soon be out interviewing for employment.

I know you are thinking this is pretty basic again. That is because marketing is basic. It is easy to identify what needs to be done. What is hard is making yourself pick up that telephone and making the first call or getting in your car and calling on that first business. There are a million reasons why you can not today, but you will do it first thing tomorrow. But tomorrow never comes.

While interviewing Sun Specialists, Inc., Skip told me he called on a particular retail store every Friday for two years before he got his first order. The retail drug store was the largest on the beach and he made deliveries along that beach route every Friday so it only took an extra fifteen minutes to stop, say hello, and ask if he could be of any service. *"When the owner finally gave me an order, I was speechless."* Skip went on to say that the owner has since become a personal friend and one of his largest accounts. What is the moral? Remember the fairy tale about the hare and the tortoise? We are trying to build a home-based business that will provide a base of clients and friends that will endure. Perseverance is the key to success. If you make those twenty five calls a week, you will generate all the leads and future customers you need.

In the interim, write those newsletters on an ongoing basis just to keep your name in front of your client base. Think in terms of twice a year and print twice as many as you think you will need. One to mail and one to hand out as a marketing piece for the next six months.

As a final thought, do not purchase a preprinted newsletter from a commercial service and have your name printed on the cover. It is apparent that the newsletter was commercially printed and they are usually too generalized to market your specific services. Write your own newsletter based on your knowledge, your products and services, and tailored to your customer base.

6. **PUBLISH A PAMPHLET OR BOOK**: A published book also creates tremendous credibility and adds to your credentials as an established authority. Books may initially appear kind of foreboding and threatening, but we are not talking about a thousand page novel with two years of research. We are talking about a "**How To**" book. For example, one entitled *PROFILES IN INDEPENDENCE: STARTING A HOME-BASED BUSINESS.*

The secret is to write about your specialty area. Write about your experiences. Write about unique or timely topics going on in your field of expertise. It is the same concept as an article, except expanded. To give you another example, one of the sample articles was "Six Ideal Plants For Low Maintenance Landscaping." Why not expand it to a pamphlet or book entitled *LOW MAINTENANCE LANDSCAPING: NATURAL FLORIDA PLANTS.*

There could already be a book like that. I only picked it as an example because I worked on the yard all weekend and keep threatening to try low maintenance, never water gravel. If you think I am teasing drive into St. Petersburg, Florida sometime and check out some of the waterfront homes. No grass. But the gravel comes in all colors from artificial grass green, to tan, to multi color. Green for the lawn and red gravel for the flower garden. If you write the book, I will buy the first copy.

The publication can also be any size you want from a pamphlet with fifteen or twenty pages bound with a staple in the middle and a soft cover to a medium size book with a couple of hundred pages or more. Published with a paperback cover in 5½ X 8½ or 6 X 9 inch format, you can have the book printed yourself at a reasonable cost. The concept of self-publishing or desktop publishing from a home-based office is one of the fastest growing areas in the publishing industry. The alternative is to try and find a publisher who is willing to incur the cost of printing, advertising, and distribution. For your purposes in publishing a How To book, to use as a marketing tool to enhance your reputation, the most likely avenue is to plan on having the book published yourself.

During one of the interviews, Sheryl Nicholson talked about self-publishing *Working Women are Working Wonders*, a 5½ X 8 inch paperback with 111 pages to enhance her professional speaking and training seminars. It is a delightful book and not only adds to her credibility but provides an additional source of income as it sells for $12.95 and has gotten her live interviews on local television and radio talk shows.

I know all this sounds like a lot of work, but keep in mind you do not have to do it all the first week. Remember the part about having a balance between work and play. I will admit, however, the first year or two I probably averaged seventy hour work weeks. The hardest part is getting established. Once you have built up a client base and established name recognition in your target market, maintenance is a lot easier.

7.   **MAILING LISTS**: Assuming you have acquired a computer or worked with a desktop publishing business and prepared a professional looking flyer or brochure, printed on a laser printer, what do you do now? You have two choices for acquiring a mailing list and preparing a mailing. The actual mailing is easy, by the way;

WordPerfect as well as most other word processing software, contains a mail merge function which allows you to merge a mailing list with a customized letter. Each letter is personalized with the name and address included in the mailing list. Even envelopes or address labels can be mail merged. Unfortunately, you still have to lick the stamp or rent a postage meter from the U.S. Post Office. Although I have to admit, I have occasionally wanted to ask the postal service to lick the stamps.

The mailing list can be compiled based on a simple listing of all your business contacts and potential customers which you are aware of or by researching your public library for directories which contain listings of potential customers. If your customer base is local, try the Chamber of Commerce for a listing of members in each city which you want to do business in. Most will either provide the listing free, or in all likelihood charge a small fee for it. Many professional associations will also provide you a listing of their members for a fee. Some will even provide the listing printed on address labels. If you plan to do repeat mailing, you might even ask for the listing on a diskette.

The last resort is to purchase a mailing list which someone else has compiled. Mailing lists usually sell based on a cost or rental per 1000 names. I use the term rental, because most mailing list agencies specifically state they are providing the mailing list for a one time use. I use the term "last resort" only because you do not know how good the mailing list is that you rent. In many cases, the mailing list agency has access to literally millions of names and you have to provide the search parameters for the specific list you are looking for. There is no guarantee that the names are still at the given addresses, will fit your needs, or are even breathing.

My recommendation for most home-based businesses is to do the research to develop your own mailing list. In addition to saving the mailing list fee, you can ensure the mailing list you compile is the most accurate and "on target" list that you can come up with. Given the cost of postage, expense in preparing and printing the marketing flyer or brochure and investment of your personal time in preparing the mailing, you want mail delivered to qualified customers. Mail that a corporation is unwilling to deliver and puts in the garbage or the post office is unable to deliver is kind of expensive.

TRUISM #8: PUT A FIRST CLASS STAMP ON YOUR MAILING. DO NOT USE THIRD CLASS MAIL RATES.

The last thought in your mailing is to put first class stamps on your advertising. I know third rate or bulk rate is about one half the cost, but I have done a fair amount of bulk mailing and it is a pain. First of all, the rules you have to follow in compiling the mailings to meet the postal service guidelines with respect to bundling the mail by three and five digit zip codes is irritating. In addition, when you hand the post office that box with 4,000 mailings along with a pretty reasonable check for postage, instead of being pleased to see a customer as most normal business would be, you have just ruined their day. Their friendly smile is replaced with a growl and you end up thinking, *"If I ever come back here again, it will be too soon."* I will assure you that if postal delivery is ever deregulated the existing U.S. Postal Service will last about fifteen minutes. That is on the generous side. If you are reading this and you work for the Post Office, this is the Customer Satisfaction Survey which I forgot to send back.

The second reason to avoid bulk rates is that delivery takes forever. I have called potential clients and existing clients (some personal friends) to follow up on a bulk mailing to have the party say, *"What flyer?"* or *"What brochure are you talking about?"* At first, I thought it was just a way of saying they had not read the flyer or they had thrown it away, but when friends and long term clients say they did not get the mailing then I began to wonder. In many cases, it would be three weeks or so before they would get the mailing. I do not know why it takes so long to deliver the mailings except the Postal Service must have known what they were doing when they called it "bulk mail" or "third class" mail.

The last reason not to use bulk mail is that if you are mailing to large corporations, I have been told by friends that in a number of cases, large corporations have instructed their mail rooms to throw away bulk mail. They consider bulk mail to be mostly unsolicited advertising and they do not want to incur the cost of distributing it through out their organization.

If you are going to go to the expense of preparing first class marketing literature, you might as well use a first class stamp.

MASS MARKETING

Now that we have discussed marketing to a specific market which we can readily identify, let us shift to a mass market in which everyone is a potential customer for your product or service. Now what do we do? Some of the same marketing techniques will work but others will have limited value.

1. **PERSONAL REFERRALS AND BUSINESS CARDS**: Just as in personal marketing, personal referrals are still the best source of leads. Keep telling everyone you know or run into what you do. Print up an interesting business card with something to make it stand out and give one to everyone you meet. *"Oh, let me give you a card in case you need to call sometime,"* should be the ending of every conversation you have.

No mater what you pay to have the cards printed, the cost is nominal on a per card basis. Sure, a lot will get thrown away, but a lot will get passed on to a referral or saved and filed in a business card case for future reference. To give you a couple of examples based on our Profiles, Skip Moore with Sun Specialists, Inc., hands out a business card with a photograph of a beautiful girl with a gorgeous tan in a T-Back bathing suit at the beach. Superimposed on the picture is the name *Hawaiian Tropic* since Skip is the distributor for Hawaiian Tropic tanning lotions on the Florida West Coast. On the other side

of the card is his company name and address. The business card is eye catching, done in excellent taste, and makes you smile when you think of Hawaiian Tropic; which is exactly what the card is intended to do.

Balloonies, another profile, has a great business card. The background is gloss white and is covered with colored balloons connected to dangling strings which lead your vision down to the company name *BALLOONIES* with the owner's name and address under it. It's great! Because they attend bridal shows, Michele said they average a thousand cards a month. If there is anyone in our town who has not heard of Balloonies, I haven't met them yet.

2. **YELLOW PAGE ADVERTISING:** With the whole world as your market, yellow page advertisements are an excellent and economical way to introduce your products or services to the public. As a consultant, I have probably received two calls from my yellow pages listing in eight years and absolutely no business. Of course, I don't expect to get calls from the yellow pages because clients do not tend to look up consultants in the phone book. Consulting is a personal service business and does not lend itself to yellow page advertising. I am only in the yellow pages because I automatically get a one line listing because I have a business phone.

For mass marketing, however, yellow pages are an excellent source of advertising. How many times have you looked in the phone book for a specific service? We all do, because it is convenient. For example, I needed a locksmith who provided 24 hour mobile service on a Saturday night at 9:00 P.M. Just where do you think I found one? To be honest, I did not really want one. But the neighbors around one of my rental homes were going absolutely crazy over an alarm system that had been going on and off for the last day over loud speakers hooked up in the garage. The renter was out of town for the weekend and the neighbors had called the sheriffs department but they could not enter the home without the renter or owner being present. They finally reached me to come over with a key. It would have been easy but the renter had changed the locks!

Was my wife happy to find a 5" by 8" yellow page advertisement that said, "24 HOUR MOBILE SERVICE - LOCKED OUT - FAST SERVICE - LOW RATES" and had a picture of a van with a locksmith logo on the side? Was I happy she found that yellow page advertisement, while visiting with a group of highly irate neighbors who were not leaving until the alarm was either turned off or the speakers smashed into a million little pieces?

The less personal your service or product is, the larger the yellow page advertisement you need. The locksmith is a good example of what I mean. Although a skilled locksmith is required, as a consumer, I do not differentiate among locksmiths. They can either do the job or they can not do the job. If I don't perceive the difference between an adequate locksmith and a highly skilled one, then I am going to call whichever advertisement catches my attention. So put in a large ad with boarders, a couple of graphics, and some different sizes and styles of fonts.

3. **SELF PROMOTION**: The term self promotion is used for lack of a better term. As a home-based business, the idea is that you have to find as many ways to reach as many consumers as possible in an economical manner. You have to get your product into their hands. Your customer has to visualize or experience the benefit of using your product or service. As a small business, it is almost impossible to use newspaper advertising in an effective way. This is because newspaper advertising is incredibly expensive and does not have a lasting impression. If you will start noticing the newspaper advertisements, the commercial advertisements seem to be from the same companies week after week.

The reason the same advertisements appear is that the companies have entered into annual contracts with the newspaper committing to a certain volume of column inches in exchange for a substantially reduced rate. In addition, the repetition of the advertisement is to build name recognition and enhanced credibility with the reader. In most cases the advertiser is a very large retail outlet, department store, or a chain of stores which can spread the advertising cost over a large base of sales.

For example, when D & B Credit Consulting started, the first thing Dennison did was run a commercial advertisement. He did not get a single call. It is not the type of advertisement we look for as we read a newspaper.

How then do we reach a mass audience? Get out and meet as many potential customers as you can. When BALLOONIES started, one of the first things Michele did was put on a clown outfit and attend every flea market, parade, celebration, or fair she could find. Any gathering of people she could find, this smiling clown was there selling helium balloons for $2 each and passing out business cards. Not only did she make money selling the balloons, but soon everyone knew the name BALLOONIES and knew she also did birthday parties, easter baskets, and would deliver balloon arrangements for any occasion. You could even pick between the clown outfit, a gorilla outfit, or an easter bunny outfit. The point is, Michele created her own marketing promotions. What do you think would have been the response if she had simply put an advertisement in the newspaper that said, "Balloon Arrangements: Clown, Gorilla, or Bunny Costume - Will Deliver." You guessed it, I do not think she would have gotten a single call. You can not read about what she does. You have to see her. The customer has to be able to visualize the fun and the excitement when a smiling clown or huge black gorilla comes into an office delivering a Balloon Arrangement on someone's birthday.

When Skip Moore started distributing Hawaiian Tropic, it was a brand new product so retail stores were reluctant to inventory the suntan lotion when no one had ever heard of it. To create demand by the beach crowd, Skip and his wife began going along the beach offering free suntan lotion. His wife would pass out suntan lotion out of a large squirt bottle and tell the kids to ask for Hawaiian Tropic at the local retail drug stores. Consumers began asking for Hawaiian Tropic so the stores began carrying the product. As the stores began to inventory the lotion, Skip kept compounding the growth by hiring additional girls to pass out more free samples. Again, the marketing point is that you have to get your product or service in the hands of the consumer. You can not just run an advertisement or send out mass flyers.

To give you a couple more suggestions or ideas on getting your product in the hands of the consumer, think about the automotive industry. This might not be the best industry to use as the industry credibility is not too high, but I can recall driving my first new Porsche. I had been driving an older Porsche so I had gotten to know some of the sales people at the dealership. As the new model year began and I was in looking at the new cars, the salesman told me to take one home for the weekend and see what I thought? No high pressure, no credit application to fill out, no contract to sign, he knew me so he just gave me the key. Did his marketing strategy work? What did my two teenage boys think when I showed up with a new Porsche in the driveway? You already know the answer, I told you in the introduction about buying a brand new Porsche.

Let me contrast that approach with a local Dodge Dealership. Just this last year, Dodge introduced the Stealth, the Dodge version of the Mitsubishi 3000GT, so I drove the Porsche down to the Dodge dealer to look at the car. It is a 1985 Porsche, so I told the salesman I was thinking about a newer car and would like to test drive the Stealth. The salesman looked at me, put his thumbs in his belt, and said, "*NOPE! The only person going to drive that car is the person who buys it.*" I probably stood there with my mouth open, because he went on to say, "*If you want to write up a purchase contract, we'll get it approved, and make it subject to a satisfactory test drive.*" I can not recall what I said, but I am sure it was not very nice.

I thought it was just me, but I have a friend who drove a 1989 Toyota Supra to the Dodge Dealership and asked to test drive the same Stealth. The sales person told him the exact same thing. I do not think he was as polite as I was.

Let me give you another marketing idea for a service business. As you know, I have a home-based business and travel quite a bit teaching corporate computer leasing seminars. As a result, my lawn is probably the worst in the neighborhood. Since my two teenage sons are now in college, I have lost my only access to forced labor as my wife told me to stuff it. As I have sat here working on the computer, watching the grass get longer out of my living room window (now an office), and contemplating a lawn service, guess who pulls up across the street every Thursday and mows the neighbor's lawn. You guessed right, a home-based lawn service. They have never left a card, a flyer, a pamphlet about the importance of lawn care, or rung the doorbell to ask for my business. They have to know my yard needs mowing because they are not blind. I know that for a fact because they have never hit any of the neighbor's trees while mowing the lawn.

If they really wanted to do some creative marketing how long would it take for them to just mow my yard and leave a nice brochure on my doorknob with a note on the back saying, *"Looks like you've been busy at work, so we thought we'd help out while we were mowing your neighbor's yard across the street. We're here every Thursday. If you would like a quote on lawn care, we can give you a very attractive rate since we don't have any additional travel time."* I have watched the riding mower they use. It must have a 48 inch cut, so they could probably mow my yard in thirty minutes. Figuring $10 an hour for labor, it would be equivalent to a $5 sales call.

If they didn't want to mow my yard, as an alternative, how long would it take to place a nice flyer on the doorknob of every home in the neighborhood? My neighborhood has fifty homes in it and thirty five lawn mowers fire up every Saturday morning at 9:00 A.M. It sounds like the beginning of the Indianapolis 500.

Repetition and dependability are the keys. We actually contracted with a lawn service once. He showed up four times and we never saw him again. We heard from the friend who referred the lawn service that he went back to college. The lawn service that mows the lawn across the street is there every Thursday like clockwork, but nobody knows who they are.

4. **TRADE SHOWS:** Local Trade Shows are an excellent opportunity to meet a high volume of potential customers on an economical basis. Notice I said, local trade shows, I have found that national trade shows become substantially more expensive due to the additional cost of air travel and lodging. In addition, shipping advertising and display material to an out of state location is an extra expense and something always gets lost.

If you do decide to attend national trade shows or trade association conventions, pick the city carefully and read the convention times reserved for the exhibitors. We once exhibited at a leasing annual conference in Las Vegas. The exhibition was almost empty except for the exhibitors, so we talked with each other. Where were all the convention attendees? It should have hit me earlier before spending all the money to fly out computer equipment and two associates to work the booth. The convention attendees were in Las Vegas to "party" not to attend conference meetings and view exhibitor booths.

We also exhibited at a trade association meeting in which the exhibition hours were during lunch and after the days meetings. All told, the exhibition booths were available about three hours a day for two days. The scheduling which resulted in a huge attendance during lunch for about thirty minutes and at the end of the day for about 45 minutes.   Lunch was scheduled from 12:00 P.M. to 1:30 so the attendees came into the exhibition hall for a half hour after they had eaten lunch and before they went to the 1:30 meetings.   In the evening, the attendees came in from 4:30 to about 5:15 and then headed to their rooms even though the exhibition hall was open until 6:00.   During the day when the exhibition hall was not scheduled to be open the doors were locked to encourage participants to attend the association meetings.   The exhibitors, meanwhile, stood around with only each other to talk to.

I just attended a local Computer Exhibition at our Civic Center and it was excellent.   The exhibitors had scheduled seminars throughout the day on specific topics of interest as well as having approximately seventy five exhibitors displaying their products and services.   We went to the exhibition during lunch and stayed for the rest of the day.   I am confident the participants felt the benefit in being an exhibitor was worth the investment because the attendees were there because they wanted to be.   They were not there as part of a national convention or professional association conference.

To give you another example, in an earlier section we talked about BALLONIES, and Michele's nonstop marketing.   One of the ways in which Michele increased her business in providing balloon arrangements for weddings was through exhibiting at Bridal Shows. Not only does Michele attend and decorate her exhibition booth, she provides balloon decorations and arrangements for the entire Bridal Show.   This gives her a chance to display her products and, at the same time, provides the future brides an opportunity to visualize her balloon arrangements at their upcoming weddings.   In fact, the exhibition booths are probably complimentary in exchange for providing the Bridal Show balloon decorations.

5.   **FARMING**: No, we are not talking about a home-based vegetable garden, although the concept is not too far off. We are going to discuss a marketing technique in which we take a mass market and break it into manageable parts. As I originally heard the concept it was used in a real estate brokerage context, so I will use that industry as the example. If the concept originated somewhere else then my apologies for not giving the originators credit.

The farming concept is very simple. As we evaluate our home-based business and begin to identify and segment the potential market, in some cases the sheer market size itself is intimidating.

Consider the bewilderment facing a new real estate salesperson. Where does a real estate salesperson even begin to determine where to acquire listings of homes to sell. The potential marketplace is only limited by geography. The whole city and every surrounding bedroom community are potential clients. The farming concept, therefore, is to identify specific neighborhoods to concentrate on, or "farm" as the concept implies.

The idea is to simply become an expert on the specific neighborhoods which you have identified as your market segment. I have even heard of cases, where real estate offices have even assigned neighborhoods to individual sales people in order to avoid duplication of effort among the sales people. The basic concept is to initially send introductory letters to all the residents in the neighborhood offering personal attention in satisfying their real estate needs. The initial contact is followed by periodic mailings or personal visits providing information about homes for sale in their neighborhood, sale prices of homes which have sold, free appraisals if they are thinking of selling, information or trends effecting values in their neighborhood, and etc.

The keys to the success of the concept are specialization and repetition. Repeated mailings of flyers or newsletters on a periodic basis gets the home owners used to seeing the sales persons' name which they will hopefully begin to associate with a specialized knowledge of their neighborhood and with a sales associate who is not here today and gone tomorrow. The real estate industry in particular is flooded with part time agents and sales people who enter the industry with visions of easy work and big sales commissions, only to go back to a regular job when they find out the industry is very competitive and hard work is required to make a living.

The same specialization or farming concept can be applied to marketing our own home-based business. The first step is to take an unmanageable market place and break it down into manageable markets or neighborhoods. For example, break a metropolitan area into segments based on their zip codes, or specific communities. If you are looking for a listing for names, addresses, and phone numbers most every town has a Cross Reference Directory which identifies residents by address as well as by name. It is not a random phone call when insurance agents call every person on a specific street.

The next best source of information is the public library. I was doing some mailings a few years ago looking for apartment units to buy (back before the real estate crash). The public library had microfiche listing every apartment complex in the county along with the owner's name and addresses. Where do you think the property data and information came from? From the county property tax records. The apartments were even indexed alphabetically by owner, by street address, or numerically by tax folio number. Just for fun, I looked up my name. Sure enough, there I was with every piece of property recorded in the country records with my name on the deed.

If you are looking for specific mailing information start with the library. Ask the librarian for help. That is there job, and I have usually found they go out of their way to be helpful. If you do not want to do the work, start asking around and you will be amazed how many small businesses exist which will provide detailed mailing lists to you.

So far, we have talked about mailings to our specific target markets or "farms." However, we can expand from mailing marketing literature to personal visits and novelty items. For example, I have another friend who started a real estate brokerage company. Not home-based, but his marketing concept was unique. He named his brokerage company after the specific neighborhood which he wanted to specialize in. He then coordinated the company name, his company logo and his marketing to identify with that specific neighborhood. He even had coffee cups imprinted with his company name and logo. Every person who entered his office got a coffee cup. His wife owns a florist shop, so he put a flower in each coffee cup, tied a ribbon around the handle, and went door to door introducing himself and passing out coffee cups. If I recall, his specific target market had about two thousand homes in it, so it must have taken him a while.

I also have a Florida Real Estate Broker's License and a few years ago I sold one of the residential rental homes which I own. Do you think I sold it myself? No! I listed it and sold it through the Realtor I was just telling you about. Do you want to know why? I only have my license because I buy an occasional investment property. I knew when it came to residential sales, he would do a more aggressive and better job marketing that home than I could. Plus, I do not have one coffee cup, I have two coffee cups!

The point I am trying to get across is that you can not market to the whole world. Break your market into manageable pieces and go after it. Let them know you are in business. It does not really matter if you send them a flyer, a newsletter, give them a coffee cup, have a clown deliver a helium balloon, or mow their lawn. But, do something to get your company name in front of the customer. If you use a mailing, do not mail just once. Put them in your computer's data base management software and periodically send a mailing. The repetition and follow up is what separates you from your competitors.

I had my teeth cleaned a couple of years ago at a dentist's office that I do not normally use. A friend was working there and she did the cleaning. I do not just let anyone play around in my mouth! She has since left, but this dentist has the best mailing program I have ever seen. Not only do I get reminders for my six month cleaning and a checkup, I get an occasional newsletter telling me how important dental hygiene and preventive dental care is. The dentist even has his receptionist call to follow up the cleaning notice to schedule an appointment. It is only my absolute fear of a dentist which has saved me so far!

6.   **COUPONS**:   For mass marketing in a specific neighborhood or manageable market segment, coupons are a great idea. Inserted or printed in a local newspaper or booklet like the "Shopper", they provide an inexpensive way of reaching a large number of customers. The key is the selection of the local publication. If you can only support a specific geographical area, do not pay to have your coupon delivered outside your market area.

The absolute best example I can think of in our local area is Little Caesars Pizza. I can remember when the local franchisor opened his first store in November of 1982 and started advertising with "two pizzas for the price of one" coupons. Nine years later he has twenty five pizza stores. I do not even know where all the Little Caesars Coupons come from, but they are all over my house. I wanted to make sure I spelled "Caesar" correctly, so I headed for the refrigerator. Stuck to the refrigerator wall with a little magnet shaped like a Pepsi can were eight coupons. I counted them! I turned around and there were three more Little Caesars Coupons staring at me from the breakfast bar with some crazy guy yelling "Lotsa! Lotsa!" I was embarrassed, I know my sons come home from college on the weekends and put the coupons there so they will have something to eat. I can not possibly eat that much pizza.

Coupons are a great idea. Depending on your product or service, however, you need to decide what kind of coupon to use. As a consumer, I think the most effective are the "buy one get one free" coupons which a lot of restaurants use. I am also involved in the ownership of a self-service car wash and we used free tokens when we originally acquired the business as a way to increase visibility. We passed out tokens to all our friends and at apartment complexes in the surrounding area. The token was good for four minutes of time. On the average, we found that most users take eight minutes to wash their car by the time they rinse, soap, scrub, and rinse again, so each free token used actually generated $1 of revenue for the second four minutes. I will admit, however, we discontinued using tokens and converted the coin meters to cash only, when my partner showed up one day to wash his car and a teenager offered him car wash tokens for a quarter each. The tokens turned out to be washers which the youth bought by the pound at the local hardware store.

If your product or service is a repeat product and the cost is low on a per time basis, a coupon for one free product is very effective. We have already talked about the lawn service mowing my yard as a marketing effort. What about the same concept applied to other businesses? Could a commercial cleaning service offer one month of free office cleaning based on a twelve month contract? If the customer is not satisfied, they can cancel the contract at the end of the first month at no charge.

Could a house cleaning service offer a free 1 hour house cleaning? Sure a few people would take advantage of the coupon, but would it generate additional long term customers? The point is to get potential customers to try your product or service. The quality and value of the service has to keep them coming back. The coupon is to entice or encourage that first usage.

Coupons which I think are the least effective are the $1 or $2 off coupons. Coupons should present an irresistible offer if the customer has any interest in the product or service. As I look at an occasional coupon, if I do not have any interest in the product or service, the coupon immediately goes in the garbage. If I do have an interest, I will save the coupons which offer a free trial or sample product. If the coupon only offers a $1 or $2 off or fifty cents on a grocery item, I just throw them away. The amount of discount just is not enough to make me want to save the coupon and then try to remember where I put the coupon when I am ready to go shopping.

7. **CENTERS OF INFLUENCE**: In many target markets the potential customer base may be large or small, but due to the nature of the product or service, may share a common interest and common centers of influence. For example, if you are providing a tennis related product or service and you have identified your target market

as existing and potential tennis players, the local tennis clubs are clearly centers of influence. If you offer a non-competing product, you will want to have your business card and a brochure on your product available to tennis players at every tennis club or center of influence in the area.

What we mean by a "non-competing product" are those products or services not offered at the center of influence. If you are offering racquet stringing, do not bother to ask a local tennis club if you can pass out a brochure offering your service when the tennis club already offers racquet stringing services. If you go to the local city parks which have tennis courts but do not have a tennis shop or tennis professional, placing your business card on a bulletin board would certainly be acceptable. If you offer tennis lessons, leave a pile of business cards and brochures with all of the retail stores in your area selling tennis equipment as you are offering a complimentary product or service not a competing product.

At every veterinarian's office in the area, you will find a card from Brenda Saling offering dog obedience training. You will also find that same business card at every pet store in the area as well as dog obedience training classes sponsored through several pet stores. Are they complimentary services? The pet stores have a vested interest in making sure their pet customers are satisfied and pleased with the services offered through the pet store. Even the veterinarian has a vested interest. Do you think they prefer a well trained, well behaved dog or the alternative? Do they charge you extra if you bring in a dog who thinks his name is Garfield instead of Odie?

One question which you will have to decide on your own is the issue of referral fees. In some cases, centers of influence may ask for, or you might think of offering a referral fee for mentioning or "*referring*" complimentary services. You have to decide how you feel about this issue. From a professional standpoint, some professions prohibit this practice. For example, Certified Public Accountants are prohibited from accepting referral fees for referring business to other professionals such as banks, lawyers, insurance agents, etc. Real Estate Agents are also prohibited from accepting referral fees from title insurance companies, mortgage companies, insurance agents, etc. For non licensed professions, however, referral fees are a matter of personal ethics and business practices.

A distinction should also be made if the center of influence is providing a service such as actively marketing your products, sponsoring a workshop, or providing meeting space for your service.

This could even be a marketing technique for your business. Offer to provide a workshop, or class, or series of lessons with the center of influence co-sponsoring the service. Since the center of influence will be involved in marketing the service they should participate in the profit or derive some tangible benefit. If you have not met the person before and he or she is not familiar with your service, offer a free workshop as an introductory service which the center of influence can offer to his or her existing customers as an additional service. Since it is a marketing sample, limit the scope of the offering. For example, a veterinarian might send a flyer to his existing customers offering a free two hour dog training clinic based on a drawing of six participants from those who respond. If the veterinarian sent out five hundred flyers, that is exposure to five hundred potential clients and the cost is two hours of your time.

As an alternative, offer to provide a special discount to existing customers of the veterinarian. If your normal dog training workshop is $100 per participant, offer a special rate of $59. Use the veterinarian facilities and hold the workshop in the evening. You gain additional customers and the veterinarian gains the goodwill associated with providing an additional complimentary service to his customers at a savings.

In some businesses, complimentary samples are an accepted practice. For example, if you will notice in a golf or tennis club, the club professional often wears the same brand of clothes as the shop sells. Or, the club professional may play with the same brand of racquet as the club store sells. In many cases, these are complimentary, and provided by the clothing or racquet manufacturer.

CONSISTENCY

Now that you have gotten a pretty good idea of some marketing ideas, do not get excited and spend your whole marketing budget the first month. Consistency is the key in advertising. Get your potential customers used to seeing your name.

I have been advertising for probably seven or eight years in a specific trade journal in the leasing industry. As I have read the journal and reviewed the advertisements over the years, it has been interesting to observe the number of companies who advertise for just a couple of issues and then the advertisement disappears. Let the reader know you are in business for the long term.

The same concept applies to flyers and brochures. A one time mailing will get a response, but repeated mailings will develop a long term business relationship. I recently conducted a seminar for a particular Fortune 100 company at their annual kick-off sales meeting for the year. It was great. They held the sales meeting at a beautiful beach resort and I was scheduled for a four hour workshop. When they initially booked the workshop, however, they started the conversation by calling and saying, *"OK, Gene, we're ready to do business now."*

They had seen my advertisements for years, I had sent mailings, and even made a personal marketing call while in New York for a seminar with another company. I flew in early and stopped at their company to talk about their training requirements. It was probably a year after that visit, that we finally conducted a workshop.

In another situation, while on a consulting engagement to evaluate the potential acquisition of a company my client and I made a trip to meet with the management of the company. As my client and I were meeting the company management, my client began to introduce me when the company president stopped the introduction saying, *"Oh yeah, the Software Man."* It was the first time I had met the company, but they knew my name from advertisements for our PC based Leasing Analysis Software which my brother and I had developed and marketed through Gene Pike & Associates, Inc.

The point is, people read your marketing literature and often save it for future reference if they have an interest in your service. The best way to capitalize on this interest is to develop a specific target market, a systematic mailing program, and follow up your mailings. For example, I have about a 1,000 companies which I mail to that are members of the American Association of Equipment Lessors. If I break that membership into monthly mailings, I can mail out about a hundred marketing brochures a month and in ten months every company has heard from us. Since most of my marketing literature is prepared and printed in my office, the cost is easily less than $1 per mailing so if I budgeted $100 a month for direct mail, every potential customer would receive one mailing a year. If I got really energetic and budgeted $200 a month for direct mail, then every company would hear from us about every six months and I still do not have to work during December. (I have already explained about balancing work and leisure.)

If you recall Don Pressler with Pressler & Associates, Inc., he has a specific target market of about two hundred petroleum distributors. He could send a monthly flyer or newsletter on new product announcements and the cost would be less than $100 a month. Direct mail does not have to be expensive if you target your market and do most of the flyer preparation yourself. There is a reason we bought that computer and laser printer.

Lori Reeves with The Flyer Service, recently told me she had 4,000 flyers printed on her flyer delivery service. Since she is in the business of delivering flyers for other companies, she included her own flyers while making deliveries to each stop on her delivery routes. She prepared the flyer on her Apple Computer, had it commercially printed for less than $200 and incurred no postage. She said she has been getting so many calls she hides when the phone rings.

CONFIDENCE

The last and most important issue in marketing is to keep a positive attitude. Remember marketing is a numbers game. Rejection and "no" is an everyday occurrence. You have to keep marketing in a business context, rejection is not personal.

In many cases the customer may have an interest in your product or service, but the timing is not right. View each sales call or mailing as a long term investment in customer development. Do not get discouraged. Set a daily goal to make ten calls or send ten brochures. Set aside the time and make yourself write one **HOW TO** article for your local newspaper in the next thirty days.

Pretty soon your efforts will start to generate leads and the leads will result in sales. You will also find the leads and sales result in referrals and your customer base starts to expand. Ask each customer how they heard of you? If they were referred, send a "Thank You" note to the customer who referred them. If you use coupons or flyers, keep a copy with a note reminding yourself where or how they were distributed. Pretty soon you will get a feel for the advertising or marketing that works best for you.

CHAPTER 4

BUSINESS SELECTION

One of the hardest questions many people face as they contemplate the start of a home-based business is what business to start? I used to ask myself, *"What do you want to do when you grow up?"* The problem is that I am not sure I have ever grown up. I have grown older, but I am not sure that is the same. We all grow older, and at different times during our lives we have different needs and aspirations. Our motivation and satisfaction levels change as these growth stages occur.

As you think in terms of your business aspirations, one of the questions you need to address is, *"What are you dissatisfied with in your current position?"* If you are thinking about a home-based business, you must be missing something. Do you want to be your own boss? Are you dissatisfied with the amount of money you are making? Do you have a problem with your current boss or co-workers? Are you tired of managing other workers? Are you just bored with doing the same job day after day? Do you enjoy your job, but you are bored with going into the same office and the same surroundings every day? Do you just want a new challenge?

You might think these are rhetorical questions, but you have to address them before you jump up and start a home-based business. What are you looking for? As you assess your own situation, one of the key questions you must answer is whether you are willing to continue doing the same type of work you are doing now, or do you want a total change?

If you are satisfied with your technical expertise and just want the challenge and freedom of a home-based business the transition is much easier. If you want to totally change your direction into a new field, the road is pretty rocky. To give you a feel for the businesses profiled in this book, the following list highlights their transition to a home-based business:

COMPANY	TECHNICAL SKILL
A-Team Cleaning Services	New
Balloonies	New
C & S Crane Service	Same
D&B Credit Consulting	Same
The Flyer Service	New
Globe-Con	Same
Me Kit Training	Same
More Than Survival	Same
Pate Accounting	Same
Paradise Vending	New
Photographics	Same
Pressler & Assoc.	Same
Rising Star Productions	Same
Royal Palm Planning	Same
Salings Obedience	Same
Sun Specialists	New
Walsh & Assoc.	Same

Of the seventeen companies profiled, twelve utilized existing skills which they had acquired through technical training and experience in a corporate or job environment. The remaining five entrepreneurs started new business ventures in which they basically had to start from the ground floor. Of the five, however, Paradise Vending was actually a combination of existing technical skills and a significant capital investment. The other four were business ventures which did not require specific technical skills but primarily relied on marketing to make the businesses successful.

After interviewing the entrepreneurs, there seems to be a direct correlation between technical skill and ease of entry into the business. If you have a technical skill or specialty area which you are marketing, competition seems to be less and the chance of success higher. For example, a commercial cleaning service has a lot of competitors because entry into the business is relatively easy. Anyone can start a cleaning service. The keys to success are providing a quality service and personal marketing to get and retain customers. In the case of A-Team Cleaning Services, the technical skill required was not high, but the partners already had a base of potential customers due to their visibility, personal friends, and existing contacts in the area.

In the case of Balloonies, Michele has seen lots of competitors start up and close down because anyone can start a business and sell balloon arrangements. The cost of materials is nominal and almost no capital is required to start the business. What has made Michele successful? Marketing. Michele is so full of life and enthusiasm you can not help but buy balloon arrangements from her.

It is the same with The Flyer Service and Sun Specialists. The entrepreneurs succeeded because they were determined they were not going to fail and worked until they did succeed.

TRUISM # 9: UTILIZE AN EXISTING EXPERTISE AND BUILD A BUSINESS BASED ON YOUR CURRENT SKILLS.

The first step in this self analysis is to assess how you are currently making a living. What does your current employer pay you to do? Be specific and make a list. Do not list generalized management. If you are a manager, what do you manage? What skills do you utilize in your present position? Which of those skills do you enjoy the most?

When I originally planned to start a business, I assessed my own background. I had a technical financial background, had been in financial management with responsibility for budgeting, pricing, financial planning, and treasury operations, and also had corporate and college experience teaching financial management. What did I like best? What did I like the least? What did I not like about the corporate world?

I realized I did not like routine daily operations. For example, being a Controller or Accounting Director with corporate responsibility for recording revenue and expenses, getting the employees paid each month, and preparing monthly financial statements was not what I wanted to be. I decided I did not like managing a large staff. I liked the analytical challenge of working with just a few people on a specific project, until that project was done and then going on to the next project. I wanted the freedom to work my own schedule. I am like the computer programmer who works fifteen hours a day for two months to finish a project and then wants to go sailing for two weeks. I liked teaching financial management and developing my own course material. In front of a class, my personality completely changed. It was exhilarating!

You have the idea, asses your own likes and dislikes. Can you take one of your current skills and build a home-based business around it? If one company will pay you for your current skill, why not get ten companies to pay you for that same skill? If you want to test the transition to a home-based business, offer to work twenty hours a week as a consultant for your company. Offer a one year contract at half pay and see what they say.

My brother did that to work with me in developing a PC based Leasing Asset Management Software program for leasing companies. At the end of the year, his company hired him back full time by making him an offer he could not turn down and I could not hope to match. What have you got to lose? You have a year to test the market for your skills and a financial safety net because you are getting half pay. If you can not live on half of your current pay supplemented with your savings for a year, do not even think about starting a home-based business. You do not have enough financial savings. If you are afraid they will not hire you back full time at the end of the year, forget about a home-based business, you do not have enough self confidence!

I have not met an entrepreneur or home-based business owner yet who was not willing to bet his job that he would succeed. I once read that an entrepreneur is someone willing to work 12 hours a day to avoid an 8 hour a day **JOB.**

FRANCHISES:

As you evaluate your own skills, you will probably also evaluate potential franchises advertised for home-based businesses. In reviewing the franchises, it would seem that part of the value of a franchise would be customer recognition obtained through national advertising. In addition, most franchise programs should have equipment packages, marketing plans, and training programs in place to provide initial help and ongoing support.

If you are looking at home-based franchise opportunities, they should meet these criteria. In addition, another criteria which you should consider is an assessment of how the franchisor generates their revenue. Do they generate revenue primarily from the initial one time charge for the sale of the franchise, or from an ongoing percentage of sales?

If the franchisor is committed to building your franchise and actually feels there is long term potential to be successful, the bulk of their revenue should come from on going franchise fees and not a large one time purchase price. Do not be lulled into thinking you will save all the future franchise support fees by paying a large fee to purchase the franchise. If a franchisor wants a large initial fee in relation to the equipment included in the franchise, it should immediately make you suspicious. If you are going to make a long term commitment, the franchisor should also have the same level of commitment.

You may already have the impression that I am a little skeptical and not a big proponent of home-based franchises. You are right. I always question what I am potentially buying? If the idea is so successful, then the franchisor should want to be in business with you for the long term. It's your money, but I would look real long and carefully, before laying down a large chunk of savings for the intangible value of a franchise. Money is very hard to save, but it is very easy to spend!

I will also admit that I am the first to eat my words if I am wrong, so if you have an "all american, red hot, can not miss," home-based franchise opportunity, send me a copy of the marketing literature. If it turns out you are right, I will buy you dinner the next time you are in Tampa.

SPECIALIZATION

I occasionally access an on line computer service like Prodigy or CompuServe in the evening to get business ideas, computer comments, and generally recharge my business batteries. I enjoy reading user questions and responses in the "Working From Home" Forums from other home-based businesses.

All too often, the following appears: "WORK WANTED, mother with small children has home computer, would like to work at home in order to be here with my children. Any suggestions. What should I do next?" Or, the message sometimes reads, "Fortune 500 manager, frustrated with corporate career, looking for home-based business ideas. Would appreciate any help, ideas, or business opportunities."

The answers and responses to the above are always interesting and usually pretty vague. The reason the responses are vague is that you are the only person who knows your business experience, technical skills, and aptitude. A computer is just a tool. What you do with the computer is a totally different issue. You can answer advertisements all day long from the back of business opportunity magazines for home computer work and you will never make a dime. Companies are not going to pay you to stuff envelopes or send you computer work from a magazine advertisement.

The first thing you have to do is figure out what you know how to do with the computer or what your technical skill is? What is the Fortune 500 you work for currently paying you for doing? Building on the home computer idea, what software can you use? Can you do mailing lists? Can you do desktop publishing of flyers or newsletters? Can you do graphics work? Whatever your specialty, you have to define what it is you want to do, become proficient at that technical skill, and then start marketing your services.

If you sit waiting for the phone to ring, you will soon be looking for a job. Assume you define desktop publishing as your technical niche. Do you have the equipment and software to do commercial jobs? You have already read Chapter 2, you know what it takes. Given that you do, what should be your first brochure? Your own. Make the best brochure or newsletter you can as a sample of your work and start marketing. Go back and read Chapter 3 again. If you still do not know where to start, read it again. The point is you have to define the business and you have to make it work. That is the whole objective of a home-based business.

Do not plan on a single revenue producing job for the first couple of months. Start making those phone calls. Mail those flyers and brochures. Get in your car and make those personal calls. If you still do not know where to start, pick up the yellow pages in the phone book and start with A. When you get to Z, start over.

Specialize. Try to pick a unique product niche to get into. Do not say you do word processing. What does that mean to a potential customer?   Tell the customer you specialize in "custom designed marketing brochures and flyers." Or you specialize in direct mail marketing with a personalized marketing letter to every business listed in your local Chamber of Commerce. How long will it take you to make a mailing list of the local Chamber members? Once you have it on the computer, how many times can you sell a direct mailing to the members. The customer does not care about the technical aspects of "mail merge." They care about a product or service. Show them a sample letter with a personalized salutation printed on a laser printer using quality stationary. Then give him a quote based on a cost per hundred letters and ask for his business.

What kind of jobs have you had for the last ten years? Take those skills and build on them. In one background interview, the individual had a corporate finance background and was responsible for preparing financial budgets and proforma financial projections for potential business investments. When he was ready to start his own business what do you think he decided to do? His home-based business develops Business Plans to assist small companies in their strategic planning and to secure financing. What do you think his future plans are? Get creative, what would you do? He plans to get a mortgage broker's licenses so they can start charging a fee if his company secures the financing. Now they have tied in the Business Plan and the financing. What next? What would be the possibility of an annual consulting contract to provide financial consulting and operations reviews? What about business brokerage, or finders fees for securing investment partners or mergers?

Let your own background be your guide. You do not have to have a corporate background. My son and I just restored a 1973 Datsun 240Z. What would we have paid to have a mechanic come to our home for just a couple of hours and help us while we were figuring out how to install a new engine? It was a little too late to stop and take the car to a repair shop when the old engine is on the garage floor and the new one is hanging from the engine hoist. By the way, what do you do with the extra parts when you finish? They must go somewhere! If you have a mechanical background, could you start a business making house calls.

Sandy and I recently attended a franchise trade show, and a mobile oil change franchise was being marketed that operated out of a mobile van. The van was so fancy I was afraid to ask what the Franchise cost? Great concept, but why purchase a franchise? Why not just buy a Ford or Chevy Van without the fancy equipment and paint job? While you are at it, why not replace brakes, do tuneups, etc. at the customers' home?

In fact, almost any service business that you can think of can probably be operated out of a home-based office and a van to visit the customer's site. Even if you do the work in your office, you still need to pick up the job from the customer. Picking up the work, keeps customers from coming to your home, provides an extra service, and the customer does not even need to know your office is in your home.

BUSINESS LICENSE

Do not forget that you do need to operate with the appropriate Business Licenses as required in your city or county. In addition, you will need a State Sales Tax number if you sell a product or your state collects sales tax on a service. In the next chapter we will get into business structure, accounting, and income tax guidelines. We also touch on complying with any zoning regulations.

CHAPTER 5

ACCOUNTING & TAXES

Accounting for a home-based business is actually pretty easy. Just put the revenue in the bank when it comes in and try not to spend it too fast. As the revenue comes in we can keep track of what products or services generated it, and as we spend it we can keep track of where it goes. That is all accounting is. It must have been an accountant who gave you the impression accounting is hard.

Of course, we can make accounting hard! If you enjoy chaos, just keep one checking account and use it for all your business and personal transactions. When you get a receipt throw it away or just stuff it in a shoe box or in the bottom drawer!

The secret to accounting and record keeping is to just take a few minutes and get organized. Establish a routine so when you pay bills you follow the same steps each time. When revenue comes in we will do the same.

TRUISM # 10: KEEP SEPARATE CHECKBOOKS FOR YOUR PERSONAL AND YOUR BUSINESS USE.

Now that you have a separate business checkbook, we can get started. This might seem like a simplified approach to accounting and record keeping, but it works. Because it works and it is easy, I will pass the approach along. In addition to having a business checkbook, you also need to buy an accordion style file folder. You can either use one which is divided into monthly sections or alphabetical sections. Personally, I recommend the alphabetical sections. Label the last section **"Cash Expenses"** because you will rarely use the "XYZ" section.

Next, when you open your business account, get a business or commercial checkbook not a personal style checkbook. A business style is about 9" by 14", the checks come three to a page, and there is a header to each check which you use to write the date, a description of the check and to balance your checkbook. Business style checks are more expensive than personal style checks but the additional cost is worth it.

Now we are ready to pay some bills. As you sit down to pay the bills that come in, get your business checkbook and your accordion file folder. Write the check and fill out the business check header so you know who the check was made out to and what it was for. Then take the invoice and write on it "PAID," "CHECK # XXX," and file the invoice in the monthly section or alphabetical section of your file folder. The alphabetical sections are preferred because you can file the invoices by company name incase you need to look them up. If you have them filed by month, you have to remember what month you paid the bill. As my editor reviewed this chapter, I noticed a big red "Not By Month" written in the border. A former IRS Auditor, Sandy said she never asked for receipts for a specific month, but always asked for documentation to support a yearly total for a particular subject such as repairs. File your receipts and invoices alphabetically, and you already have them all together.

The next step is very important. When you purchase anything for your business with cash, a personal check, or a personal charge card take the receipt and write on the back what it was you bought or what the business purpose was. Do it when you pay for the item and put the receipt in your wallet. As soon as you walk in the door when you get home, go to your accordion receipt

file folder and put the receipt in the section you labeled "CASH EXPENSES."

Do not put the receipts in the glove box of your car, on the bedroom dresser, or in your pants' pocket (the ink comes off when they go through the washing machine). Receipts go in your wallet or purse and then in the file folder.

The next step in record keeping is to deposit the revenue. With a business checkbook you get separate deposit books. The deposit books have deposit slips which are white and yellow and come with a little piece of carbon paper. Use the carbon paper. The white deposit slip goes to the bank and the yellow copy stays in your deposit book. The yellow deposit slip copies become a permanent part of your business records. All revenue goes into the deposit book, cash does not go into your pocket. If cash does go into your pocket, you will find the IRS has a very limited sense of humor. The deposit ticket will become the source of our accounting so identify the deposits as best you can. If you have multiple checks to deposit, list each check separately by company name. Under the company name write what the check was for. For example, I write "Seminar," or "Consulting," or "Software Sales," etc. If you have a lot of small sales and you do not keep track of individual invoices that you send out then just write "Misc. Sales."

When you get your bank statement at the end of the month, balance your checkbook. I know that sounds simple, but how long has it been since you balanced your personal check book? How much were you off? Try not to carry blank business checks in your wallet. Your checkbook will only balance if you record the checks you write in the checkbook. Once the checkbook balances (or you are close) take each canceled check and tape it to the check header in your checkbook. I know this sounds odd, but if you leave your canceled checks in the envelope with the bank statement, you have to have a filing system so you do not lose the statements. I have done enough tax returns and asked for enough cancelled checks to know *"I can't find them"* is the standard answer. If you tape them back in the book, I guarantee you wont lose that cancelled check because the checkbook has all your canceled checks and checks which you have not written yet. Besides, the book is too large to lose. You also know if you have an outstanding check because there is a blank spot where the cancelled check should be. If you want to see if you have paid a bill, you know exactly where every cancelled check is. In fact, the checks are laid out by check number and in chronological order.

To keep from losing the bank statement and to keep it with the checks for the month, I staple the bank statement to the last check in the checkbook for the month in question. If I need to find my March bank statement, I just turn to the last check I wrote in March and there it is. The only thing I don't keep are the white bank deposit slips which the bank returns. I do not keep them because I have the yellow copy still in the Deposit Book.

The system is simple and it works. I always have my cancelled checks and I know where to find my bank statement. If I need to find a receipt, I know it is in the alphabetical section of my accordion style file folder. If you have a better system, or a record keeping idea which you find helpful send me a note for the next book.

ACCOUNTING

Now that our record keeping is under control, we are ready to begin keeping track of our revenue and expenditures by category. For this, we really need a basic accounting program for our personal computer. Probably the most well known home accounting software on the market today is Quicken by Intuit Corporation. It can be purchased at any computer software store or ordered through the mail for around $35 so the cost is nominal.

The key to a computer based accounting system is to keep it current by entering your deposits and expenditures each month. Get in the habit of paying any leftover bills at the end of the month and then doing your accounting. Quicken will even print your checks for you if you order customized check blanks. Personally, I just write the checks by hand but if you are concerned with a very professional appearing check Quicken is certainly an option. I usually figure most vendors are just happy to get a check and the last thing they do is look to see if it was hand written.

The process of starting an accounting program starts with establishing a Chart of Accounts for your revenue and expense categories. A Chart of Accounts is just an accounting term for the list of categories you want to use in tracking your revenue and expense items. If you decide to use Quicken, it comes with a standard Chart of Accounts for small businesses. The Chart of Accounts can be modified by the user by adding, deleting or changing any of the categories. Their Chart of Accounts can be numerical or alphabetical, but most accounting software only accepts numerical account codes. It is also a lot easier to enter a three digit code rather than type in an account name. As an illustration, the following slightly modified Chart of Accounts from Quicken is provided (including sample account numbers):

CHART OF ACCOUNTS

INCOME:
- (400) Gross Sales
- (410) Other Income
- (420) Rent Income

EXPENSES:
- (500) Advertising
- (510) Car and Truck
- (520) Commissions
- (530) Freight
- (535) Interest Paid
- (540) Legal & Professional Fees
- (545) Late Payment Fees
- (550) Office Expenses
- (560) Rent Paid
- (570) Repairs
- (575) Returns & Allowances
- (580) Taxes & Licenses
- (585) Travel Expenses
- (590) Wages & Job Credits
- (595) Insurance

If you will notice, Chart of Account categories usually have a consistency built into the numerical scheme. For example, all the revenue accounts begin with a 4 and are three digits. All the expense accounts begin with 5 and are three digits. If you expand your Chart of Accounts you can also have subaccounts within your categories.

For example, you might have three advertisers that you use in promoting your business. If you want to keep track of how much you spend with each one, you could identify account (501) Local Newspaper, (502) Technical Trade Journal, and (503) Direct Mail Flyers. Let your imagination and personal business requirements be your guide.

At the end of each month, right after we balance our check book, we will also account for our specific revenue and expense items. Start up Quicken or the accounting system you elect and we are ready to start entering the revenue. For each deposit, write the account code on the deposit slip, draw a circle around it, enter the deposit into your accounting system, and then put a check mark or your initials on the deposit slip. This tells you that you have entered the deposit in the computer.

Then do the exact same thing for each check that you wrote. On the check stub, write the account number, put a circle around it, enter the check in your accounting system, and put a check mark or your initials on the check stub. Get in the habit of doing it the same way each time.

As you are entering the account categories some of the checks will not be for expenses but are to purchase assets or pay off loans. For these items we need to expand our chart of accounts to include assets and liabilities:

CHART OF ACCOUNTS

ASSETS:
     (100) Cash - Checking Account
     (101) Cash - Money Market Account/Savings
     (110) Loans to Employees
     (120) Office Furniture
     (130) Office Equipment
     (140) Accumulated Depreciation
     (150) Other Assets

LIABILITIES:
     (200) Payroll Taxes Payable
     (210) Social Security Taxes Payable
     (220) Loans Outstanding
     (230) Sales Tax Payable

OWNERS EQUITY (CAPITAL STOCK):
     (300) Capital Stock (Corporation)
     (310) Owners Contribution (Personal)
     (330) Net Income (Retained Earnings)

With these asset and liability accounts, we can prepare a net income statement each month to see how much profit we made (or lost). We can also prepare a balance sheet to reflect our assets and liabilities. As you are reading this section do not get concerned with the mechanics of entering the revenue and expenses in your accounting system. The software manual that comes with your program is usually pretty good about helping you set up the accounts and showing you how to enter the data. Quicken probably built its' reputation based on how easy it is to use.

ACCRUAL VERSES CASH BASIS ACCOUNTING

Another thought for you to think about or at least be aware of is the difference between accrual accounting and cash basis accounting. Before you get too concerned, however, with the use of accounting terms it is a lot easier to use cash basis accounting as a small home-based business.

To illustrate the difference, assume you charge a customer $1,000 for a job which you just completed. Because the customer works with you on a regular basis, you normally send him an invoice when you finish. In accrual accounting you would record $1,000 as revenue (credit) and increase your accounts receivable balance (debit) by $1,000 when you finish the job. Later, when you receive the $1,000 payment you would increase your cash balance (debit) and decrease the accounts receivable balance (credit). If you will notice we increased accounts receivable (debit) and then we decreased (credit) accounts receivable by the same amount when we got paid.

Most small businesses do not want to worry about accounting for a transaction until they get paid. As a result in cash accounting, which is an accepted method of accounting, when we finish the job we do not record anything. We do not record the revenue until we get paid. When that check for $1,000 is in our hand and we are rushing it to the bank, then we record $1,000 as revenue (credit) and increase our cash balance (debit). The end result is the same and cash accounting is a lot easier.

If you use cash accounting, it will also make your income tax return a lot easier as we will have to make a few adjustments but they will be minor. One caution, however, if you sell items which you inventory the IRS requires that for your tax return you use accrual accounting.

PETTY CASH

Petty Cash is an item which is difficult to manage and even more difficult to account for. To solve the record keeping problems, do not use a petty cash account.

The easiest way to keep track of small purchases is with our "**Cash Expenses**" file in our accordion file folder. All of the expense receipts in the balance of our files have been paid by company check and the check number is written on the invoice or receipt. By definition then, all the receipts in our "**Cash Expenses**" file are from personal cash expenditures, a personal charge card, or a personal check.

Each month as you do your accounting, or before if you need the money, add up the receipts for the "**Cash Expenses**" which you have put in the file. Write yourself a business check for the "**Cash Expenses**" total. Then staple the receipts together and write on the top receipt, "REIMBURSED,   CHECK # XXX,   DATE XX/XX/XX." When you account for the reimbursement check at the end of the month just record it as Office Supplies, Travel, Lodging, Meals, or whatever most of the receipts were actually for.

This treatment, by the way, is essentially the same as what happens in a large corporation. As an employee, if you incur business expenses you make out an expense report and the company writes you a check as reimbursement for the expenses you incurred. When I write a check to reimburse myself, I even go one step further. Instead of writing on the top cash receipt, I actually make out an expense report. I itemize each business receipt on the expense report and then staple the expense receipts to the expense report. This might be extreme, but it is due to my training in GTE Corporation. I even use their expense report form, I just overlaid my company name and made a copy of it. I hope expense report forms are not copyrighted.

The next part is a little tricky, but what happens if you do not have the cash and you need an advance for a business trip or a number of small business purchases? If you will look back at the sample Chart Of Accounts, there is an account under assets called (110) Loans to Employees. This account could also have been labeled Cash Advances. If I write myself a check as a cash advance for a trip, the business is really making a loan to me for the amount of the cash advance. Record the check by decreasing (credit) cash and increasing (debit) Loans to Employees.

When you get back from your trip make out an Expense Report, staple the business receipts to it and put it in your "**Cash Expenses**" file. At the end of the month add up all the cash expenses, but instead of writing yourself a check for the total amount, only write a check for the difference between the Cash Advances and the total for the expense receipts which you have. For example, if you have written yourself $300 in cash advances and you have $330 in receipts, the business owes you $30. If you only have $250 in receipts, you owe the business $50.

To account for the expense report and all the receipts for cash expenses, instead of writing yourself a check for the exact amount, record (debit) what the expenses were for and then reduce (credit) the Loans To Employees account. Keep in mind the accounting system you are using will take care of the mechanics of debiting and crediting, but you need to understand the concept of employee advances and submitting expense reports or receipts for cash expenses as reimbursement.

Of course, the easiest way to avoid having to account for cash advances would be to not have any and just submit expense reports for reimbursement. But, who has any cash?

INCOME TAXES

To begin a discussion on federal income taxes we first need to have a basic understanding of business structure. As an additional observation, this section is intended to give you an overall feel for corporate or business federal tax guidelines, but it is not intended to be all inclusive or to substitute for professional tax advice from a Certified Public Accountant, an Enrolled Agent, or a Tax Attorney.

TRUISM # 11: YOUR TAX ACCOUNTANT SHOULD BE YOUR MOST TRUSTED FINANCIAL ADVISOR.

In this section, I have also avoided any discussion on state income taxes because every state is different and the last time I counted we had 50 of them. As an additional reference, which is available at no charge (you do make a small contribution each April 15) call the IRS and request IRS Publication 334 Tax Guide for Small Businesses.

BUSINESS OPTIONS:

As a small home-based business, we have several options which apply to us. First, we can operate our business as a sole proprietorship which is essentially a business owned by one person and not incorporated. A sole proprietorship is taxed as a self-employed person and uses IRS Schedule C to report income and expenses. The nickname for this business is a "Schedule C" business due to the IRS form used. As a Schedule C, you are liable for all debts of the business including any litigation or suits against the business.

If you have decided to incorporate, you have three options. One is a regular 1120 corporation in which the corporation is treated as a separate tax entity. The second is an 1120S, or "S election", in which the corporation elects to have the income or loss of the corporation flow directly to the personal income tax return of the individual stockholder(s). The third election is a Personal Service Corporation which is essentially a 1120S Corporation, except any gains or losses are defined as passive. Personal services are services in the fields of law, health, engineering, architecture, accounting, actuarial sciences, performing arts, or consulting. The concept of a personal services corporation was introduced to prevent passive losses from being passed through to personal income through the use of a corporate structure.

The corporate nicknames, again come from the IRS Forms. A regular corporation files its' return using IRS Form 1120 and if you make the "S" election you use IRS Form 1120S.

SOLE-PROPRIETORSHIP

This form of business is the simplest and easiest to start. The cost is nominal and unless you are worried about personal liability, is probably the best when you are first getting started. As you begin to get some business and start to feel confident that your business will succeed then you might consider incorporating.

About the only legal requirement to start is a business license in most areas and the registration of a fictitious name if you are using a name other than your own. The business license is a matter of paying a fee and insuring you comply with any local zoning requirements about the use of your home. Because every city or county has different rules, you will need to find out what your local requirements are. Having said that, in most cities you will probably find there is some restriction against operating a home-based business. You can apply for an exemption, or in many cases individuals just ignore the zoning requirement.

Now, I am not suggesting that you ignore the zoning regulations, I'm just saying that most home-based businesses probably do. As long as you are not generating traffic by selling a retail product out of your home and employees are not coming to your home everyday you probably do not have a major concern. However, if someone reports your business to the zoning commission you may have to comply with the zoning guidelines, move your business, or request a zoning variance. Keep in mind, in most areas there is a distinction between a home business and a home office. If you simply maintain a home office as a place to work in the evening that is different than a home-based business. Should you ever have a problem, think about moving your business address to a friends business which is located in a regular commercial office and just maintaining a "home office" instead of a home-based business.

You may also want to register your fictitious trade or business name with the state you live in if you want to make sure no one else is using it. I don't think this can be done on a national basis, but in Florida you can register a fictitious name by recording the name with the state, advertising it in the local newspaper one time, giving the public seven days to respond, and then getting a certification from the newspaper that you announced the fictitious name in the paper.

Schedule C: Profit or Loss From Business

Expenses: If you are self-employed, report all expenses possible using Schedule C not as Job Expenses or Miscellaneous Expenses on Schedule A of your personal tax return.

Tax Year: Your tax year for your small business will generally be the same as your personal tax return.

Self-Employment Taxes: As a sole-proprietorship you are responsible for paying self-employment taxes on your net income (Schedule SE). Keep in mind you may already be paying employment taxes on income from another employer. For 1991, self-employment taxes are broken down into two parts: 12.4% of your net income up to $53,400 for taxable social security wages and 2.9% of your net income up to

$125,000 for Medicare. This is a combined rate of 15.3% of the first $53,400 of net income or wages and 2.9% of any excess up to $125,000.

To eliminate the penalty self-employed individuals used to pay because the corporate portion of employment taxes is a tax deduction to a corporation, the IRS has calculated an adjustment factor which is applied to net income. Before calculating the self-employment tax you owe, multiply your net income on IRS Schedule C (Line 31) or Schedule SE (Line 2) by .9235.

For example, if you had net income of $30,000 from your home-based business and did not work elsewhere, your social security taxes would be ($30,000 X .9235) X 15.3% or $4,239. In addition, you would get to reduce your taxable income on Form 1040 (Line 25) by one half of the Social Security Tax of $4,239. One half of the Social Security Tax of $4,239 is $2,119. Assuming you are in the 15% income tax bracket, this will reduce your income taxes by $318. The net of all this is that on $30,000 of net income, you effectively pay ($4,239 - $318) $3,921 or 13.07% in social security taxes. If all this seems complicated to you, do not feel like the lone ranger.

Assets: (IRS Form 4562) You also need to remember to make a distinction between expenses and capital investments. If you are buying an asset then the asset must be depreciated rather than expense the purchase. For a small business, however, congress did help us out with a special election.

Section 179 Election: You may elect to expense up to $10,000 of the cost of certain business equipment in the year you purchase and place the equipment in service (Schedule C, Part II, Line 13). For example, as a small business you purchase office equipment totaling $6,300 during the year. You can elect to deduct the entire amount instead of depreciating the purchase price.

This election also applies to automobiles, but the maximum deduction in the first year is $2,660 of the automobile cost. For a more detailed discussion on autos talk with your tax accountant.

If you purchase more than $10,000 of equipment then you can elect the full $10,000 Section 179 deduction and then depreciate the balance of the cost of the equipment as if it were another piece of equipment. There is a limitation, however, in applying the Section 179 election. The $10,000 Section 179 election is based on filing a joint return and it may not exceed the net income from all your active businesses.   This election also applies to corporations and partnerships.

Depreciation: Except for the Section 179 Election, assets purchased during the year or in prior years must be depreciated based on the depreciation rules in place when the equipment was placed in service. For example, if you bought equipment in 1991, you would follow depreciation rules using MACRS (Modified Accelerated Cost Recovery System) Depreciation guidelines.

MACRS generally provides for 3, 5, 7, 10, 15, and 20 year lives for equipment purchases depending on the type of equipment. For most small businesses, the five and seven year categories will primarily be used. For example, the five years class life includes computers, typewriters, automobiles, trucks, copiers, and computer-related peripheral equipment. The seven year class includes office furniture and fixtures such as desks, files, cellular phones, and fax machines.

For a more detailed discussion of depreciation, get an income tax guide or call your tax accountant again. I hate to keep referring to other sources, but I wanted to give you a small overview of tax considerations without writing a whole book just on tax guidelines.

Active Participation: (IRS Publication 925) If your business has a loss, to offset active income from another job you must materially "regularly, continuously, and substantially" participate in the business. If you do not materially participate then your business is defined as a "Passive Activity" and the losses can only be use to offset income from other Passive Investments.   There is a seven part list of questions which the IRS uses to determine if you materially participate. You only have to meet one of the seven tests.

In our case, this is not a significant concern, because we will be actively involved in our home-based business. In addition, we plan to generate profits and not losses. This is one of the more complex of the IRS areas, so if you have any doubt that a loss is active or passive, definitely see a good tax accountant. If you generate a profit, don't worry about whether it is active or passive unless you have other "passive losses" which you would like to use to offset active income.

Office in the Home: (IRS Pub 587) As a home-based business you have the right to deduct part of the cost of operating your home as a business expense. This expense, however, has not been viewed very favorably by the IRS and it is my impression that they have made it as difficult as possible to qualify for the deduction. In addition, this is one of the areas that I am convinced will help to trigger an audit.

To deduct expenses for a home office, two tests must be met. You must use your home-office "exclusively" and on a "regular" basis in one of the following two ways: your office must be used as a place of business to meet or deal with patients, clients, or customers in the normal course of your business, or, your office is your principal place of business if you spend most of your working time in your office. If you have another job where office space is available it is very difficult to qualify for this deduction.

If you want to claim this deduction, I would recommend that you have a separate room set up and used as an office for your business. If you are trying to use a desk in your bedroom or the dining room table after the dinner dishes are cleared away you are just inviting an audit. An audit which you will lose since your office space is not used "exclusively" for business. As a separate thought, if you claim an office in the home, I would make sure that the rest of your return is "squeaky" clean. There is nothing more irritating that to hear the IRS auditor say, *"While you are here, why don't we go ahead and take a look at* ______________? It is called Expanding The Scope Of The Audit, and the agent has every right to look into other areas on your return.

Remember, you must use the office space on a "regular" and "exclusive" basis. You might convince the auditor that you use the dining room table on a regular basis, but it would be a tough sell to convince the auditor that you use it "exclusively" for business and not to also eat dinner at.

If you have a separate room which you use to store inventory which you sell, that space also counts as part of your office in the home. Apply the same "regular" and "exclusive" test. If you use part of your garage, it's a tough sell. If you have inventory in the closet of your bedroom which has been converted to an office it adds to your credibility.

The IRS also has an income test for your office in the home deductions. Your office deductions cannot exceed the net income of the business before deducting the office expenses. To illustrate this assume your business had a net income before office deductions of $1,500. You can only deduct home office expenses up to the $1,500 limit. Any excess office expenses are then carried forward to future years, subject to the same net income limitation.

Assuming you do meet the IRS guideline for office in the home and you want to claim the deduction, the following will give you a feel for what is deductible and how to calculate the percentage of your expenses allocated to your home office. There are two methods of calculating the allocation percentage of your expenses. The first method is to calculate the square footage of office space as a percent of the total square footage in your home. For example, a 12' X 12' bedroom would be 144 square feet or 8% of the total space in a home with 1800 square feet. If the rooms are equal or approximately the same size, then you can allocate expenses based on an allocation of total rooms. For example, if your home has seven rooms and you use one for business then your business percentage would be 14.29%. I will tell you the IRS prefers the square footage allocations method because most bedrooms are smaller than the other rooms in most homes. Once the percentage is calculated it is applied to the total allowable expenses.

Allowable expenses include the following:

Rent
Interest on a mortgage
Property Taxes
Property Insurance
Utilities (excluding your residential phone line)
Depreciation (the basis of the home is the lower of the
     fair market value when you begin using your home
     for business or its adjusted basis less land cost)
Maintenance (Must generally benefit the office space)
Security System
Lawn care and landscaping are <u>not</u> deductible

Once you calculate all the expenses to operate your home including depreciation apply the business percentage to the total to derive your office in the home deduction.

HEALTH INSURANCE: Again, in order to minimize the tax differences between a self-employed individual and a corporate structure, 25% of the amount paid for health insurance coverage may be deducted. The deduction cannot be greater than the net income of the business and is carried to your personal return on line 26 of Form 1040. If you itemize expenses on your personal return the remaining 75% of your health insurance premium is deductible as a medical expense on Line 1 of Schedule A.

AUTOMOBILE EXPENSES: (See IRS Publication 917: Business Use of A Car) Automobile expense guidelines are generally a mess and a little complicated due to the limitations set in place a few years back to limit deductions for luxury cars. Generally, though you have two options in deducting the business portion of automobile use. First, if you elect in the year you place your vehicle in service, you can take a mileage allowance and not worry about tracking actual expenses of operating your car. For 1991 the mileage rate is 27.5 cents a mile.

The alternative, is to calculate the actual expenses of operating your vehicle including depreciation and then prorate the expenses between personal and business use.

A major caution, here, the first thing the IRS is going to ask if you get audited is how you calculated your mileage. The correct answer is, "*I keep a mileage log.*" Of course, to give this answer you must actually keep a log. I know that is a major pain, but if you want the mileage deduction you have to substantiate your mileage. Get a little notebook, put it in the ashtray (try not to put a match on it), and each time you take a business trip write down the mileage. If you want to save time set the odometer trip meter to zero and then write the date, business purpose, and mileage. If you really want to impress the auditor write the beginning and ending mileage also. The IRS tries to use the laundry system here. **No ticket, no laundry!** Keep the log.

If you don't keep the log, your auditor may allow you to reconstruct your business mileage if you can reasonably do so. The best bet, however, is the log. Use the log to calculate what portion of the total mileage is business and what portion is personal or commuting mileage. Remember, as a home-based business your commuting mileage is zero.

Use the business percentage to allocate your expenses such as maintenance, gas, oil, car washes, insurance, tag registration and fees, interest, and depreciation. The business portion of interest is also deductible on Schedule C as a business expense if you are <u>self-employed</u>.

Depreciation is also deductible given certain limitations. If you use your car 50% or less for business in the first year of use, then you cannot use a Section 179 election or MACRS depreciation, but must use straight line depreciation over 5 years. Even if your use is greater than 50%, your maximum depreciation per year is subject to a "luxury" limitation. If you place your car in service in 1991 the following limitations apply:

    1991: $2,660
    1992: $4,300
    1993: $2,550
    for years after 1993: $1,575

The maximum depreciation deduction for the first year also includes any Section 179 election which you take. These limitations are maximums for the year. The depreciation limit is also allocated between business and personal use. If your business use is 65% then you can only deduct up to 65% of the maximum depreciation.

AUTOMOBILE LEASING: Automobile leasing has the same basic rules as owning an automobile and using it for business. The total lease expense and costs of operating the automobile must be allocated between personal and business use. Do not get rid of that log yet. The same rules apply about documenting your business use.

Leasing also has the equivalent of the "luxury" limitation when you purchase a car. For leasing an automobile the "luxury" adjustment applies to any car costing more than $13,400. Between you and I, Congress certainly has a strange sense of humor when they think a luxury car begins at $13,400. Of course, if your congressional aid or limo driver picks you up and takes you to work then you don't have to worry about the cost of a luxury car.

If you are self-employed and deduct the lease expense for a leased car, then add back to your personal income an amount based on a table published by the IRS. This amount is allocated on the same basis as the lease expense is allocated between personal and business use. The following samples were taken from the IRS Table:

Luxury Car Leasing Table for 1991

Original Cost of Car	Income Addback
$ 13,400- $13,700	$ 2
$ 24,000- $25,000	110
$ 30,000- $31,000	169
$ 35,000- $36,000	218
$ 40,000- $41,000	267

The intent of the income addback is to adjust your net leasing expense to compensate for the depreciation limitation on owned "luxury" automobiles.

CORPORATE RETURN

1120S ELECTION: You can elect to be treated as a S corporation if you qualify. As an S Corporation, the net income or loss of the company flows to your personal income tax return and is not taxed at the corporate level. The corporation must file a federal tax return, but it is for information purposes only.

To elect S status you must meet five IRS tests, but as a home-based business you should not have any problem in meeting the tests. The five tests are pretty simple and are as follows: 1. It must be a U.S. (domestic) corporation 2. the corporation can have only one class of stock 3. there can be no more than 35 stockholders 4. only individuals can be stockholders and 5. stockholders must be citizens or residents of the U.S.

MEDICAL INSURANCE: As an S corporation, medical insurance premiums are treated the same as if the stockholder were self-employed. This means the medical insurance payments are not deducted as a corporate expense. Your personal taxable income is reduced by 25% of the medical insurance payments (line 26 Form 1040) and the remaining balance is deducted as medical expense on Schedule A subject to the income limitation.

LIABILITY: As a S corporation, one of the benefits is the same personal liability limitation as a full corporation. Personally, you are not liable for the debts of the corporation and in theory you are not liable for any suits or judgements against the company.

In reality, this is probably more of a paper benefit. From a lending standpoint, as a closely held corporation, a financial source will be very hesitant to lend the corporation funds without a personal guarantee from the major stockholder (you and your spouse) for the debt. Inventory, supplies and services, however, are often extended on a credit basis without a personal guarantee. If your business has inventory or you incur significant trade credit then the limited personal liability may be important.

From a legal standpoint, you are also not supposed to be personally liable for suits or judgements against the corporation. It might be my cynical nature or law training I have gotten from watching L.A. Law and Night Court, but it is my impression that juries and judges do just about whatever they want. If you do get sued, as a sole stockholder in a small business, the plaintiff will probably sue both the corporation and you personally. I am not sure I would count on the corporate structure for protection. However, just to absolve myself of any liability for this paragraph, go see a lawyer.

1120 CORPORATION

In a regular corporation, net income does not pass directly to the stockholders but is taxed as an individual entity at both the state and federal lever. The following are the federal corporate tax rates:

Taxable Income up to $50,000	15% Tax Rate
Over $50,000 but not over $75,000	25%
Over $75,000	34%

One of the benefits of incorporation if your business does make substantial net income is that the corporate income tax rate of 15% or 25% may be less than your personal income tax rate.

HEALTH INSURANCE: Health insurance premiums are generally deductible in full as a normal operating expense of the corporation. The 25% personal deduction does not apply.

EMPLOYMENT TAXES: As a corporation, employment taxes of 7.65% must be paid.   As an employee, you then pay the same amount. The 7.65% corporate employment taxes are a corporate expense and deductible on the corporate return.

Employment taxes are filed using Form 941 which is due one month after the end of each quarterly period. The employment deposits are made directly with your local bank using deposit slips from a Federal Tax Deposit Coupon Book which the IRS sends to the corporation. The due date of the deposit depends on the amount of the employment taxes. If you owe less than $500 at the end of the quarter, you can deposit the funds with your bank or send it with Form 941. If you owe less than $500 at the end of any individual month, you may carry the taxes over to the following month. At the end of the month if your taxes are $500 or more but less than $3,000, you must deposit the taxes within 15 days of the end of the month. If you owe more than $3,000 get out Circular E Employer's Tax Guide and figure out when the tax is due, you do not need my help.

UNEMPLOYMENT TAXES: As a corporation, you also have to pay and file both state and federal unemployment taxes. This expense is nominal and in reality is a benefit to use.   In Florida, the state unemployment tax rate is a function of the type of business you are in and your unemployment history. If I recall, my company started with .0270 times the first $7,000 of wages for each employee. Because I have not any claims for unemployment compensation filed against Gene Pike & Associates, Inc., my rate is currently .001. This means I pay $7.00 a year in state unemployment taxes.

Federal unemployment (Form 940-EZ) also has to be filed and is also based on the first $7,000 of wages for each employee. I think the tax percentage is a constant .008 or $56 for each employee.

As an employee of a corporation, I am eligible to draw unemployment benefits should I ever get laid off from work. I kind of view it as an insurance policy (in fact that is exactly what unemployment taxes are). If my business ever fails, the company will lay me off and I'll be down in the unemployment line to get my check. It is my understanding that you cannot draw unemployment if you are self-employed.

EXPENSES: From an expense standpoint, most of the operating expenses which are deductible for a sole proprietorship are generally also deductible for both S corporations and 1120 corporations. For a more detailed review or for more specific questions see you tax accountant.

BUSINESS SUMMARY: From a cost and benefit standpoint, as a small home-based business just starting out, I am not sure I would go through the legal expense and do the additional record keeping required by a corporation. I would probably start out as a sole-proprietorship. As the business grew and funds were a little more available, then I would consider incorporating and probably with a S election. The only benefit, therefore, being any potential personal liability shield offered by the corporate structure.

IRS AUDIT

Many of us dread the prospect of being audited by the Internal Revenue Service. I will admit an audit is not on the top of the "Most Fun To Do" list, but an audit is not the end of the world either. In most cases, an audit does not take long and any audit issues are resolved in one or two visits.

If you get audited keep in mind that the auditor is generally just trying to do his job. Once in a while, you will meet an auditor who is a little intoxicated with the position, but generally the auditors are underpaid and are faced with management pressure for increased case productivity. In addition to the management pressure their customers are not too happy to see them either. The point is, do not go into the interview with a negative attitude before the audit even starts.

Always keep in mind that the United States tax system operates on the basis of voluntary compliance. The role of the IRS is to encourage voluntary compliance and collect taxes in those cases where the taxpayers made an error or fraudulently filed returns. The IRS audits less than 2% of the total income tax returns filed. Even though the chances of an audit are low, most citizens file reasonably accurate returns. Just remember the fear of being audited is usually greater than the reality of an audit.

The IRS has two audit groups that you may encounter. Field Audit handles corporations and generally conducts audits at the location of the taxpayer. For the most part, they audit larger corporations and do not want to audit small businesses where the audit issues are minor. The second IRS group is called Office Audit.

Office Audit has the responsibility to audit individual returns and the audits usually take place in the IRS office. In most cases, you are initially sent a letter inviting you to come to a specific IRS office for an audit. The letter also highlights the initial audit issue or issues and specifies the records you should bring in. If you have moved since you filed your return, you can request that the audit be moved to an IRS office near your new location.

For example, the audit letter might indicate rental property, or unreimbursed business expenses, or medical expenses. Whatever the letter asks for, take in the receipts and documentation of how you calculated the deduction. Only take those records, not your entire file cabinet. Do not just throw the receipts in a shoe box and hand the box to the auditor. Try to match the receipts with the individual entries or line items on the tax return. If the audit is over a small rental property you have, make a pile of receipts for each expense item. If repairs are $687 then find the receipts that support that number, add them up on an adding machine, take the adding machine tape, and staple it to the pile of receipts.

When the auditor asks how you got the $687 in repairs, hand him the receipts with the adding machine tape. When the auditor asks how you got $921 in utilities, hand him the pile of stapled utility bills which you have totaled. If you are missing a receipt, say so, *"I'm sorry Mr. Auditor, I could only find $652 in repair receipts or cancelled checks. I must have lost a $35 cash receipt."* If most of your expenses are well documented the missing receipt is not a concern. If you have nine different expense items listed on your rental property schedule and the auditor finds you are well organized they might only verify five of the nine and conclude the audit.

The auditor generally works on the basis of probability. If most of your expense items are documented and you have receipts then probably all your records are good. Conversely, if the auditor examines three items and every one is missing documentation, then the auditor will continue the audit. During the audit only answer the questions asked by the auditor. For example you might have nine line items and nine piles of receipts to support the entries. If you know one is missing a receipt for $127 do not volunteer that information unless the auditor asks for those specific receipts.

Do not take in additional records. We want the auditor to conclude the audit. If you only have the specific records initially requested, the auditor will have to schedule a second appointment to audit any additional areas on your return. They have that option.

The auditor has the option to "expand the scope of the audit," if they feel additional areas should be examined. If you did not bring all your records the auditor must decide if the additional area or issue is worth the time and bother of scheduling a second appointment. Keep in mind, the auditor probably gets three to five new cases every day which they must audit and they probably have forty pending audits in the drawer which they are working on.

The point is, audits are not as difficult as most people imagine. On the other hand, if you do not keep receipts or a substantial amount of income is unreported, then maybe you should send your CPA, Enrolled Agent or lawyer to the audit. I would generalize that in most "horror" IRS audits, your friend "the taxpayer" only told you a few selected details. Maybe they forgot to mention the Country Club dues they are trying to deduct or that they only had half of the expense receipts. It is not your friends fault that the IRS is being unreasonable and will not accept entertainment receipts that do not have the name of the business client and the business purpose of the entertainment. And the IRS really made your friend mad when they questioned the deduction for a business car that was used 100% for business. "We all know no one really keeps a mileage log!"

AUDIT YEARS: From a time standpoint, may people are unsure of the length of time they are subject to an IRS audit. The general rule is three years from the later of when you filed your return or when your return was due. This means if you filed your 1988 return on April 15, 1989 then after April 15, 1992 the IRS can no longer go back and audit your 1988 return.

The reason I used the term generally, is that the three year rule does not apply in the case of fraud. But, of course, fraud only applies to other people and is not a problem in our case. This does not mean you can throw away your old tax returns. You need to save the returns to support asset purchases, depreciation, the basis of your home, etc. I keep all my old tax returns. This might be excesive, but they do not take up much room and if I need them I have them.

Because the length of time between when you file your return and the time you are audited can be two years, make sure you have all your receipts at the time you prepare your return. Do not think to yourself that if you get audited you will find the receipts then. The audit will be a couple of years later. You will be lucky to remember where you filed the tax return. Do all your sorting and stapling at the time you prepare the return.

Give yourself a mini audit. We already know an audit will not be "fun" but do not add to your misery with poor record keeping.

APPEALS: Without getting into a lengthy discussion on your appeal rights and legal options, it might be helpful to know that you have two appeals within the IRS that are automatic. The first appeal, if you feel the auditor has been unreasonable, is the Group Manager. All you have to do is say, "*I would like to meet with the Group Manager.*" If the Group Manager is available he will see you immediately. If he is unavailable at the moment, the IRS auditor will schedule an appointment for you.

The next level of appeal is to Appeals, a separate group which is in the IRS. Although Appeals is part of the IRS, they are unrelated to the Audits and work as a check and balance to ensure the taxpayers are being treated fairly. The objective of Appeals is to settle as many cases and issues as possible to avoid tax court litigation which is expensive for both the IRS and the taxpayer. Appeals has the authority to settle an issue in favor of the taxpayer or negotiate a settlement acceptable to both parties.

PROBLEM RESOLUTION: Another group in the IRS which you might find helpful with normal tax return issues is Problem Resolution. Because of all the negative publicity with respect to the IRS over the last decade, the IRS formed a group called Problem Resolution. Their job is to resolve issues which seem to have fallen through the cracks and the taxpayers cannot seem to get resolved.

If you have a problem which you can not seem to resolve, immediately ask for Problem Resolution. I do not know how they do it, but problems immediately get resolved. I had a specific case in which the IRS issued two identification numbers to a partnership which I formed. I filed using the first number they sent and every year for about three years, I would get a series of nasty letters for failure to file a return under the second identification number. I can not recall how many copies of the return and letters of explanation I sent to the IRS.

After finding out about Problem Resolution, I called and explained I had been given two ID numbers and could not get one of them deleted out of the IRS files. I was amazed, instead of being given six other numbers to call, Problem Resolution said they would take care of the problem and they did. I got a follow up letter from Problem Resolution a month later stating the duplicate ID number had been deleted and they were sorry for the inconvenience. I was impressed, and have not had the same problem since then.

CORRESPONDENCE: The last thought with respect to letters and requests from the IRS for information, do not ignore letters which you receive. Your patience might be worn thin and your blood boiling, but do not throw the IRS correspondence in the garbage. If you do, you will find the auditor simply disallows the expenses in question, assesses the additional tax due, and turns the problem over to collections.

You do not want to mess with Collections! These are the people who padlock your doors and put a lien on your bank account. If you owe additional taxes and do not have the money, meet with collections and work out a payment plan. Collections will usually try to work with you unless you have gone out of your way to cause problems. If you do agree to a payment plan, make your payments on time.

INDEPENDENT CONTRACTORS

Another area in which the IRS seems to have a special interest is the distinction between independent contractors and employees. As a home-based business, we are going to try and avoid having employees due to the cost of benefits and payroll taxes and the problems created if they come into your home to work.

The best way to get occasional work or specific projects finished is to contract with an independent contractor. Independent contractors are generally professionals pursuing an independent trade, business or profession. The general definition of an independent contractor is that the employer has the right to control or direct the result of the work but not the means and methods of accomplishing the result. For a detailed description of how the IRS views employees and independent contractors get IRS Publication 937, Business Reporting, and see the chapter on "Who Are Employees."

Two of the characteristics of an employee relationship are that the employer has the right to discharge the employee and the employer supplies tools and a place to work. There are several steps which you can take to lessen any potential dispute. If you anticipate an ongoing relationship have a written contract which clearly specifies the individual is an independent contractor and not an employee.

Have the individual perform the service at their location and not in your home. Have the contractor submit a written invoice for payment of services provided. Do not use a simple time sheet showing hours worked and an hourly rate.

If the IRS looks at this issue, they will look at the circumstances of the services provided and not just the contract. But if you have an invoice for services provided and you did not provide an office environment or the equipment to do the job, you should be on solid footing.

CHAPTER 6

OFFICE MANAGEMENT

This chapter is kind of a catch all chapter for a number of miscellaneous items which impact your home-based office. The first of which is the physical and psychological layout of your office. What I mean by this is that you need to have a separation between your personal life and your business life. The easiest way to do this is to have a separate room for your office. When you are finished for the day and shut the door to the office, you also mentally shut the door to your work day and make the transition to your personal life.

My wife's favorite line to start a conversation is, "*What are you working on now*?" She says she can always tell. I get quiet, my eyes narrow, a small frown forms, and if we are in the car I get 50 feet behind the car in front of me and drive the exact same speed. "*We'll be on the interstate going 50 miles an hour and you'll still be following that car*," she says.

OFFICE LAYOUT

In most of the interviews for this book, a spare bedroom had been converted into an office. This is probably ideal as it is an identifiable room with a door you can shut. (It also discourages your college age children from returning for more than a visit. As long as they have to sleep on the couch they think in terms of visiting and not moving back in.) In one case, a double garage had been converted into an office and it was ideal as it was very spacious.

In our case, we initially converted the formal living room into an office. A few years later, we converted one of our son's rooms into an office when he left for college and we needed the additional office space. The living room has been ideal as I spend a lot of time at the computer and feel closed in while in the spare bedroom. From a family standpoint, we live and relax in the family room which is physically separated from the formal living room. The living room, however, while opening off the foyer has a distinct feeling to it as it has three and a half walls and is a step down from the main level of our home.

This feeling of being able to mentally disassociate yourself from your office might seem like a trivial item, but when your home is also your office, you need a mental separation. If you are trying to work at home from the dining room table or a small desk in your master bedroom you have my sympathy.

This mental transition is not easy and has a potential impact on your family life. In one background interview for the book, the profile worked out of his home for seven years and just recently moved into a commercial office which he rented. *It's the best thing I ever did*," he stated. He went on to explain that since moving back into an office eight months ago he had lost thirty-five pounds, his two teenage daughters breathed a sigh of relief, and his relationship with his wife improved. At home, he kept making trips to the refrigerator every time he wanted a mental break and as a result started to develop a weight problem. He was home when his daughters went to school, when they returned from school and all evening. He even operated his business with only one residential telephone line, so his daughters felt like they never had any private time or privacy even for a telephone call. His wife didn't have an outside job, so she agreed to work in the home-based business.

"*It didn't work well at all!*", he exclaimed. I would ask her to run an urgent package to the post office and she would take it the next day while running family errands in order to save a ten minute trip. Meanwhile, he had told his client it was going out overnight express. He would ask her to type something or send a follow up note and she'd say, "*Why?*" He said, "*We were spending too much time together. Now, I don't get home until 6:30 or 7:00 P.M., but the time we spend together is quality time.*" Clients were also a problem if he had evening meetings at home. The house had to be clean and everyone on their best behavior which put additional stress on the family and didn't contribute to a healthy family atmosphere.

WORKING TOGETHER

Working at home is potentially difficult for either a working spouse or non-working spouse. Notice, I am using the term spouse as opposed to wife or husband, because gender has nothing to do with it. During the interviews, the comments applied to both genders. In one interview, the husband who was

in his late twenties had been a self-employed professional photographer since his college days. He had only been married a couple of years and as his wife would get up in the morning at 6:30 A.M. to get ready for work she'd say, "*Get up and get a real job. See what the world is really like.*" The problem did not have anything to do with money or the amount he was making. It was the idea that he was still laying there in bed while she had to get up and go to work. He didn't have any idea what the pressures and aggravations in a normal corporate environment were like.

My wife, Sandy was a partner in an accounting and tax preparation firm and then Fiscal Manager for a county agency until two years ago when we decided she would join me in operating our home-based business. The transition was interesting. I had been in corporate management and then got used to doing things myself. She had also been in management and had her own managerial style. We had to jointly work out our new business roles, while making sure any conflicts did not carry over into our family life.

The key to working together, or simply being home together all day, is to also have separate interests or time alone. We have already talked about getting involved in the community. Join the Kiwanis Club or the Rotary Club or any civic association of your choice. The point is to get involved in some associations where you have external social contact with peers and different stimuli. If you have business errands to run don't ask your spouse to go along just for company. It does not take two people to run to the post office or pick up stationary.

Make it a point to call a business associate, or client, or friend for lunch once a week. Don't take your spouse every time. Your spouse should do the same and develop her own circle of business associates or friends. How many times have you talked to couples where the husband retires and the total relationship changes. The wife complains that the husband is under her feet all the time. He even wants to go grocery shopping. It's great to be together, but not all the time.

From a work relationship, clearly identify separate work responsibilities. In writing this book, I wrote and Sandy edited. She was also interested in writing so she wrote the section on insurance and I edited. We both thought the process worked well.

THE REFRIGERATOR

Working at home also has other temptations which you don't have in a normal office environment. Back at the office, coffee at 9:00, lunch at noon, and soda in the afternoon were normal. But at home the refrigerator is always just around the corner. I can't tell you how to stay out of the snacks and candy, but I can suggest when you are ready for a mental break do not head for the kitchen, instead head for the neighborhood. Turn your answering machine on and take a fifteen minute walk around the block.

A walk will do you a world of good while the refrigerator will do you a world of harm. If you have made and broken eleven New Year's resolutions in a row to start jogging, now is the time. Instead of lunch, run for thirty minutes, come back and shower, and you're ready to face the afternoon. You don't have to jog, but whatever you've been putting off because you were always too busy, now is the time. Life does not get any better.

If your goal was to become a better tennis player, schedule a lesson everyday. If your backhand is nonexistent, now is the time. If you are still slicing that #5 iron, call your golf professional right now and set up a series of lessons. I have said throughout the book that the greatest benefit of having a home-based business is that you get to set your own schedule. So you take off an hour during the day. Work until 6:00 P.M. instead of stopping at 5:00 P.M. Make up for that golf lesson while everyone else is commuting and swearing at traffic. Who is going to know? More importantly, who is going to care? You are the boss.

If you just can not stand the flexibility and lack of a fixed schedule, write yourself a permanent reprimand for taking a long lunch and put it in your personnel file. Every time you are late, get out the reprimand and initial it. Also keep a list of the extra time you owe for being late. Once you get used to the flexibility and being your own boss, take out the reprimand and throw it away.

FLEX TIME

Working at home is the ultimate in scheduling your work day. We just talked about getting some exercise and working a little later. What if your biological clock thinks a rooster crowing is saying "goodnight" instead of "good morning?" I commute from my bedroom and I'm still late in the morning. But, I do some of my most productive work from 11:00 P.M. to 2:00 A.M. in the morning. It's quiet, no phones ring, there's no television, Compuserve is available at a discount, and I just like the evening hours better than working in the morning.

So I sometimes take a nap in the afternoon! There is nothing on television except for soap operas. Besides, I have to rest from my morning tennis match. The point is, you work the schedule that fits you best.

DISCIPLINE

So far, I have given you some pretty flexible office quidelines to go by, but they may not work for everyone. In my case, it's not critical that I am in the office every minute during the day because I don't get many phone calls that are urgent. Seminars are usually scheduled a month or two ahead, and if someone calls and I don't get back until the next day it's not a major problem.

The key, however, is knowing how much work you have to do. If you have a project, you have to exercise the self-discipline to ensure it gets done. If you can not function without a well established routine, then have yourself in that chair at 8:00 A.M. and stay until 5:00 P.M. You have to motivate and discipline yourself to get the job done. You know what works best for you. We are all different, so I can't provide a set of rules for you to follow.

The bottom line in my case, is the workshop which I conduct. As the instructor, if I am not prepared, the participants know it instantly. If I am not prepared and the seminar flops, the company tells me how great it went, sends a check, and I never hear from them again. If that happens too often, it's back to a normal office environment and job. I make sure I'm ready and my course material is ready. You figure out what motivates you.

PAYDAY

This next subject is also interesting and again, no gender bias is intended as the interviews were pretty evenly divided. I touched on the issue earlier in the Personal Financial Planning Chapter, but I want to address the issue again because it's critical to your success as a home-based business.

The insecurity of not knowing how much money will be available each week is a significant concern for some people. In one profile, she said her husband keeps asking her to get a normal job so he will know how much income to count on each month. She makes more in her home-based business than she could earn in a normal job but that is not the issue. *"I would rather have you earn $200 a week and count on it, than have you earn $1,000 one week and nothing the next week,"* her husband said. I suggested that she pay herself a salary each week and give it to her husband as if she were her own employee. She said that is basically what she has done. She has negotiated a flat amount each week which she contributes towards household expenses. But then, she adds, he looks in the checkbook and sees the business balance and starts pouting. She laughed when I suggested she hide the business checkbook.

In another profile, it was the wife who had trouble handling the insecurity. The bottom line, is to "Live Like A Squirrel." Pay yourself out of the business account just like a normal job. When things are going great avoid the temptation to spend the extra money. Save and invest it for when business isn't as good. After eight years of self-employment, I will assure you that each year is different and the economy goes in cycles.

PERSONAL IDENTITY

The last area which you need to think about is how you perceive your personal identity. This may sound strange, but when you meet new people how do you respond when they say, *"What do you do?"* Do you identify yourself as a member of a large corporation? Do you associate with your profession? Is you self-esteem tied to membership in a company or your corporate position? Before you answer this question, you might want to think about it for awhile.

There is no right or wrong answer. In fact, you are the only person you have to answer to. The answer, however, is critical because if your self-esteem is partly based on a sense of belonging to a collective group, then you may want to think twice about forming a home-based business. We have a friend who went to work with IBM Corporation four or five years ago. His whole world revolves around the company. If someone asks what he does, he responds, *"I am with IBM."* It is great that he loves belonging to the company.

Sandy and I are both avid tennis players and play at two different clubs. One is exclusively a tennis club and all of the members are tennis enthusiasts. In the club your sense of identify is a function of your tennis ability. You could be the President of a leading corporation or a self-made millionaire, but you are still associated with your tennis skill. The second club, is a country club with a full range of activities and memberships including tennis, golf, swimming, general fitness, and social members.

At the country club, members are a mixture of people in the corporate world, professionals, business owners, retirees, and a few that are self-employed or "consultants." It is interesting how people introduce themselves and identify with each other. Doctors instantly let you know they are God's chosen few. Lawyers are also quick to identify with their profession. In their case, I am not sure it is because they are proud to be lawyers or they are always looking to solicit new clients. Business people are a divided group. Some say they are with such and such corporation, a few identify themselves with their profession, and a few provide both labels.

The social order is a mixture of the two. Some of the members seem to associate their personal self-esteem and identity with their financial or business position while others identify with their tennis level or golf handicap. It is amazing how often a person is introduced with, *"This is so and so, he has a 5 handicap."* Tennis is a little more subtle as the USTA (U.S. Tennis Association) rating system is a little more subjective, but the association still exists. I have not quite figured out how the general fitness members establish a social order. I have not heard anyone say, *"This is so and so, he's a 200 lb. bench presser or he's a ten minute a mile jogger."*

The point is, however you identify yourself, however you measure your own self-esteem, make sure it fits with a home-based business. The social standing associated with self-employment is almost the same as unemployment. Introducing yourself as a home-based business or consultant is the same as saying, "*I am looking for a job.*" If you need the personal reinforcement of a corporate position, then do not think about a home-based business. No matter how inviting the flexibility and freedom looks, you will not be happy.

You have to generate your own self-esteem or self-value based on your own set of criteria. You cannot let others measure your success based on your financial, business, or professional position. Just to have fun with people, if they ask what I do, I always say,"*I play tennis. Work is bad for you.*" It is fun to watch as they try to figure out how I can play tennis everyday, drive a Porsche, belong to a country club, and not work. You can tell they want to ask more, but they can not figure out how to do it politely. Keep them wondering. Do not tell them all the secrets of self-employment. It is our secret.

CHAPTER 7

THE INSURANCE DILEMMA
A BANDAGE FOR YOUR BUSINESS

Now that you have read the chapters on Personal and Business Financial Planning, Marketing, and Office Management you have everything covered.   You have purchased all your necessary equipment, supplies, your letter-head and business cards are done and your marketing plan is on a roll. Everything is in place.

You have a fifteen year old son who loves to skate board. He has just been playing Michael J. Fox in <u>Back to the Future</u>, you know the part, when he is being pulled on his skate board behind a truck...Well your son being fifteen <u>and</u> a boy thinks, "*I can do that!*"

The doctor at the emergency room says that from the x-rays, a few stitches will fix him right up. On checking out with the billing clerk she asks for insurance information and you say with confidence "*Yes, I have insurance through my employer.*" Then you break into a cold sweat and wonder if your Cobra coverage has lapsed. The skateboard champion is at the University of Florida now, but if you meet him, ask if it was really his brother driving the truck?

Lack of adequate insurance coverage in this day and age is one of the quickest ways to wipe out a savings account, but what does adequate mean? Adequate means not only enough coverage for your given situation but also providing that coverage for yourself and your family at the most cost effective level.

As an employee you probably did not have any decisions to make about your insurance. The premium amount was either paid by your employer or was taken out of your check and you did not ever worry about it. Since there are no "Stop and Shop" stores for insurance where you can browse to glean some information, let us start with some general basics.

There are several types of insurance such as liability, property, automobile and health insurance. All these types of insurance can and usually should be purchased separately for either business or non-business. In some cases insurance companies will not cover business property or business liability insurance under your non-business homeowners policy. So when you start to get quotes remember you will most likely be getting quotes on two policies for each area. For liability you will have one policy for your non-business homeowners and a separate business liability policy. The same holds true for property and automobile insurance also.

HEALTH INSURANCE

If you are coming from an insured employee situation your first opportunity for coverage after you leave employment is the Cobra option that your employer must offer you. This is an option to continue being covered by the insurance your employer provided for you. Of course now that you no longer work for the company providing the insurance coverage, you will have to pay for the coverage yourself. Most Cobra coverage is available for eighteen months after you leave the company.

You will probably have to send the insurance payment to the company you worked for and they in turn will send it on to the insurance company along with the other company payments. When you sign up for the Cobra option you will be signing agreement forms to convert your insurance. In this agreement form there may be a non-payment clause that protects the company from your non-payment. Take this clause and the date you have to make the payment seriously. Cobra insurance can be a real hassle for some companies as the insurance clerk may also be handling a thousand other things. Make it easy on everyone, including yourself, by getting your check to them when it is due.

If your payment to the company is late they have a few options, none of which make for friendly relationships, as the insurance clerk will have some explaining to do to her boss.

Option #1: The company can float the payment for you until your check gets there. This means the insurance clerk will have to invest untold time and aggravation trying to get a hold of you for collection, so she can assure her boss that the company will not have to lose one months payment amount because *the check was in the mail*.

Option #2: They can send the rest of the company's payments in the hopes your check gets to them in time for them to cut a separate check to send to the insurance company before your coverage is dropped.

Option #3: The company clerk who had a very rough night up with the twins, decides not to hassle with calling you again and types out a letter notifying you that due to non-payment your coverage has been dropped. If you are dropped for non-payment, by the time the letter of notification gets to you, you have very little time, probably just a couple of weeks, to find alternative coverage.

Another important consideration before changing from your Cobra coverage, or any other insurance, that you are covered under is to find out about the pre-existing conditions limitation. The pre-existing conditions limitation is a limitation that will not cover a prior illness or condition. Our policy will not cover illnesses for the first two years that were caused by a pre-existing condition where symptoms or treatment occurred within the previous twelve months. Therefore, if

you have had an illness or injury that will require a couple of months of on-going treatment or recovery it would be wise to stay with your present insurance coverage until such time as you can wait the remaining time required to eliminate a pre-exiting condition situation. If you have a Cobra option that allows you to stay covered for eighteen months, take up to the full eighteen months if you need to use that time to eliminate a pre-existing condition situation.

Opting to convert to the Cobra plan when you leave enables you to spend an ample amount of time finding alternative insurance. The Cobra plan can also be a potential source for on going insurance, as some companies' insurance coverage can be converted to an individual plan. It would be worth the time to find out before your Cobra coverage lapses.

TYPES OF HEALTH INSURANCE

There are three major types of health insurance coverage. They are: fee-for-service (traditional), Health Maintenance Organizations (HMOs), and Preferred Provider Organizations (PPOs).

The fee-for-service plan is a plan in which the insured is billed for medical services at the full price. Based on the deductible, the insured pays for services up to the deductible amount and then the insurance company pays the balance on a shared percentage basis. The shared amount is usually 80% paid by the insurance and 20% paid by the insured, although percentages may vary. Deductibles can range from as high as $2,500 to as low as $250. The insured can choose any doctor, hospital or clinic that he prefers. This plan is highly preferred by people who prefer to select their own doctors. One draw back about this plan is that if a catastrophic illness occurs, even 20% could be a staggering amount. Check this type of plan to see if there is a ceiling amount on the 20% that you would be liable for, after which the insurance pays 100%.

The popularity of HMOs over the past few years has had its ups and downs just like any other new industry. HMOs are typically a plan where the provider has its own pool of medical services available. The services available include doctors, hospitals, clinics, and even their own pharmacies. When the insured needs medical care he must go to the group of doctors and other services available for the cost to be covered. At the time of medical service the insured usually pays a co-payment which is generally $5 to $10. This is an excellent insurance for people who tend to have numerous recurring minor illnesses or pharmacy needs. This type of insured could be a young family with several small children who need on going services such as childhood immunizations, recurring childhood diseases (chicken pox, measles, mumps, etc.) recurring colds, tonsillectomies, ear infections and on and on... This can also be a favorable choice for older people or anyone who has ongoing conditions that need regular medical follow ups and medications, such as high blood pressure or diabetes. Unfortunately we have been unable to find an insurance company that accepts individual plans. Most of the HMO carriers we talked to only insured large groups. We did find one company that would consider as little as five employees, but the premiums were prohibitive.

PPOs are a hybrid of the HMO and the fee-for-service insurance offerings. The insured usually is required to meet a deductible amount like the fee-for-service, but the amount paid for the medical service is usually a co-payment or even possibly completely covered by insurance. The medical services covered are provided by a group of doctors and other medical services who have agreed to provide their services for less in return for the listing as the insurance medical provider. This plan gives you more flexibility of choice of doctors, yet not necessarily your family doctor, at a much reduced price. Like the HMO we have been unable to find a provider that offers this plan for individuals.

LOCATING PROVIDERS

Individual coverage for self-employed people has become somewhat of a nightmare. The rates tend to be very high and in some incidents no insurance coverage at all can be found. Start by sitting down with an insurance agent to help familiarize you with what is currently available. Do not feel guilty about checking with several agents, as the policies and prices may vary even if different agents represent the same company.

If you find that individual plan prices are too prohibitive or unavailable to you, investigate group plans available also. Usually the rates will be lower and the benefits higher than an individual plan because the group generally will generate more income for the insurance company and spread the insurance risk.

Be creative in your thinking of sources available to you for insurance coverage, investigate any group you are involved in. Check with your local Chamber of Commerce for member available health coverage. Ask your related trade organizations, college alumni associations, and professional organizations. If you are eligible by age, check into AARP (American Association of Retired People) and other senior citizen groups. Military officers and dependents may be eligible through USAA (United Services Automobile Association.) See if another self-employed company wants to form a group. Consider coverage through your spouse's employer's insurance.

If you have children in college like we do, check out the student coverage available for them. It may be less expensive to cover your children under the college plan and cover you and your spouse under a separate commercially available plan.

As you investigate alternatives for individual coverage, not only do you need to ask questions about the rates and level of coverage provided, but at the same time check with your state insurance commissioner and local Better Business Bureau for any complaints that have been filed about the company. It does not do much good to have medical insurance with an insurance company who is insolvent or unable to pay their bills.

"THEY WANT <u>HOW</u> MUCH?!

After you narrow down the list of available insurance companies that may benefit you, then you can start asking the hard questions, "How much?" and "For what?"

Just as there are a myriad of options on who to insure with, there are also a myriad of options on what coverage you want and need. Do not be afraid to ask some blunt questions and be willing to push some numbers around for your best financial options.

There can be some significant considerations financially depending on your situation and what options you decide on.

TYPES OF MEDICAL INSURANCE

A traditional fee-for-service plan figures how much to charge you for your premium based, in part, on how much you decide that your deductible amount will be. Usually, the higher the deductible amount the less your premiums are. During the year you must pay for charges up to your deductible amount, then the insurance will pick up amounts over the deductible, usually based on a percentage of coverage. Such as, you pay 20% and the company pays 80% of the amount after you have paid the deductible.

It is time to get out the pencil, calculator and your mathematical aptitude. Let us look at a real life option of choices for deductibles and the premium costs involved. This example is based on a fee-for-service insurance with semi-annual premiums. The basic policy is based on a 20%/80% sharing, with a maximum out-of-pocket expense to be paid by the insured of $1,000 over any deductible amount. Once the deductible is met, any cost over the maximum of $1,000 per insured is covered in full by the insurance company. The following is a table of the deductible options:

Annual Deductible (A)	Maximum Out-of-Pocket Expenses (B)	Annual Premiums (C)	Total Possible Outlay (A+B+C)
$ 250	$1,000	$4,064	$5,314
500	1,000	3,389	4,889
1,000	1,000	2,739*	4,739
2,500	1,000	2,049*	5,549

Looking at the two least expensive premium options (*), on the chart above, if you have no incidence of illness the most you would be paying out would be your annual premium cost. The difference between the two lowest cost premium options based on deductibles of $1,000 or $2,500 is $690 ($2,739 - $2,049).

Using these same deductibles, if you had a serious illness or operation and paid the maximum your total cost for the year would be your premiums, plus the out-of-pocket, plus your deductible. The difference between the two lowest cost options then becomes $810 ($5,549 - $4,739).

So what does this mean? It means that if you elect the $2,500 deductible instead of the deductible of $1,000, you know that your savings for the year will be $690 if you have medical expenses that do not exceed $1,000. If you elect the lowest premium based on the $2,500 deductible and you have a major accident or illness the additional outlay you will incur is an additional cost of $810.

To put this choice in simple terms, you are gambling $690 to save a potential of $810. From a breakeven point, if your medical bills for the year are less than $1,862 the insurance company makes money (the $690 premium savings is 80% of $862). If your medical bills are greater than $1,862 you made the wrong decision. From an insurance or risk standpoint, I am not sure an increased premium cost of $690 is worth the potential maximum savings of $810.

Using this same logic, if you elect the minimum deductible of $250 you have spent an additional $2,015 in premiums for the year. What is the maximum potential savings? If you have a major illness you stand to save $235 or ($5,549 - $5,314). In this case you are gambling $2,105 to save $235. Does this seem rational?

If you are thinking that if you had an accident you could not afford to come with the deductible of $2,500 you are kidding yourself. You are paying the deductible anyway. You are just paying the medical deductible at the rate of $167.92 per month through the increased premium instead of in a lump sum.

TRUISM # 12: IT IS USUALLY TO YOUR ADVANTAGE TO ELECT THE LARGEST INSURANCE DEDUCTIBLE AVAILABLE.

Different insurance plans and premiums might give different results, but in the numbers we looked at, unless you were planning on a serious illness or accident the increased premium just was not worth the potential savings. One of the reasons, insurance companies need to charge a lot for policies with small deductibles is the administrative cost of processing the multitude of small claims. For example, take the $250 deductible policy. As soon as you reach $250 in medical expenses for the year, the remaining medical expenses are reimbursed by the insurance company based on 80% of the expense. This means every time you have a medical expense, the insurance company has to process a claim. It might be a $20 prescription with a reimbursement to the policy holder of $16, and the administrative and overhead cost to process the claim might average $25 per claim.

The insurance company would be better off to open a pharmacy and just give you the prescription for free. The larger the deductible, the fewer the claims the company has to process which is the premise behind Major Medical Policies. The administrative savings are passed on to the policy holders.

We have found that the traditional health plan is the most feasible option for a small home-based business or individual plan. It gives you various deductible levels to tailor your own costs and medical benefits and it also seems to be more readily available to individuals as opposed to an HO or PLO.

Up to now we have looked just at health plans, we have not considered additional plans for eye or dental care. We felt at this point it was most important to get you started on investigating health care first. Then if you have some extra dollars for insurance you may opt for an eye care or dental plan addition. For these plans also, take your time to find the right one for your situation and weigh the premium cost against the benefits received.

LIABILITY INSURANCE

Liability insurance is also fondly referred to as "slip and fall" insurance. This is a type of insurance that covers injuries to people other than your family. It usually covers all injuries sustained in or by your personal property, such as an automobile, boat, or airplane or in your home. Liability insurance can be obtained for your business and your non-business properties. The policy amounts usually run about the same cost for property of equal value. You need to realize that some insurance companies will only cover your non-business liability under your homeowners' policy and a separate business policy is needed to cover your business liability. However, some insurance companies will sell you a business rider attached to your homeowners policy. Ask which options your company can provide.

An umbrella policy can also be purchased for either your homeowners' or your business liability policies. An umbrella policy increases your basic coverage (usually $300,000 or $500,000) to the amount specified in the umbrella policy. This extra coverage will cover you against most accidents that happen either to yourself or others. The accident does not have to occur at your home. Liability insurance will usually cover you or others regardless of the location. This policy will also generally cover automobile accidents for any liability in excess of your automobile coverage up to the amount of the umbrella coverage.

PROPERTY INSURANCE

Most homeowners' policies have a dollar limit as to the value of the business property they will cover. For example, ours is $2,500. Some insurance policies will not cover property used for business at all. Therefore even though you may have adequate home insurance your business furniture, equipment and materials may not be covered. It is important, especially if you have substantial equipment, to get business property insurance. Because our homeowners' policy would only cover up to $2,500 worth of business property, we got an additional $7,500 worth of coverage as a rider on our homeowners' policy. The additional annual cost was only $1 per $1,000 of value. A very reasonable expense considering the cost to replace the furniture and equipment. If your insurance company will not insure business property under your homeowners' policy, and you have substantial business equipment you should look into getting a separate business policy.

AUTOMOBILE INSURANCE

Your automobile insurance should be adequate for your personal coverage, but you should also consider adding additional insurance to cover business related travel. Your insurance company will probably want you to get a business rider attached to your personal insurance, or possibly even a separate business policy, to cover accidents while driving for business or to cover loss of business related items from your automobile.

PRODUCT OR SERVICE DAMAGE INSURANCE

Consideration should be given to getting insurance to cover you from any claims filed against you because of damage sustained from your product or service. If you offer professional services check into errors and omissions. These types of service related insurance can be obtained through commercial insurance agents or through your professional associations. For product coverage also contact your trade associations. These types of insurance tend to be pretty expensive so again weigh the cost against the potential loss and get several different comparison quotes.

PROFILES

IN

INDEPENDENCE

STARTING A HOME-BASED BUSINESS

PROFILES IN INDEPENDENCE:

PROFILES IN INDEPENDENCE:

A-TEAM CLEANING SERVICE

COMMERCIAL CLEANING SERVICES

For the last six years, Mary Seiferd and Jan Hudgins have been partners in **A-TEAM CLEANING SERVICE**, a commercial cleaning service for office buildings, banks, and small commercial strip centers. Operating out of a home-based office, they utilize commercial grade vacuum cleaners, a commercial floor buffer, a mini van, and lots of integrity as they have built up a customer loyalty which is rare in the industry.

During the interview, I was surprised with the degree of account turnover and nature of the problems in the business. I anticipated aggressive marketing and price competition due to the ease of entry as no specific training is necessary and the capital investment required for the equipment is nominal. Instead of talking price and services to be provided, however, Jan said:

"When we first meet an account they ask are we planning on bringing our children?"

I must have looked puzzled, because she went on to explain that most of the companies in the industry hired unskilled labor to provide the actual cleaning services. Many of the employees are working mothers and the actual cleaning is done at night after the businesses have closed and before they open in the morning. With child care difficult to find during those hours, they often bring their children to the accounts. Mary went on to add that the accounts often complain of missing candy, sodas, snacks, loose change, pencils, supplies, etc., from their offices and children playing at the desks and with the office equipment.

The most important thing to the clients is the integrity and professionalism of the cleaning staff and not the price. While the price has to be within a competitive range, accounts seem to be more concerned with having a sense of trust in their cleaning service. In looking back, almost all of the **A-TEAM** accounts have come from personal contacts or referrals from existing accounts. Their clients are constantly being called and sent flyers and brochures from competitive cleaning services, but almost all their accounts have continued with them from year to year based on a handshake.

The second concern which seemed to be a major problem in the industry is the degree of turnover among the cleaning staff and the lack of dependability. Accounts constantly complained about contracting for cleaning services based on five nights a week and being lucky if the cleaning service showed up three out of five nights. If the same person showed up for three months it was amazing! This lack of dependability and turnover was a continual client concern as the cleaning employees had keys to the offices. Those clients with expensive equipment or inventory were especially concerned.

With this kind of industry image, Jan and Mary have provided a refreshing degree of dependability and integrity. Neither have children so a midnight babysitter is no problem.

BACKGROUND

With an athletic background as a nationally ranked tennis player in her teenage years, Mary Seiferd went on to play tennis for the University of South Florida where she obtained a degree in Education. Upon graduation, she went to work as the Director of Tennis at the Buckhorn Golf and Country Club outside Tampa, Florida, and for the next fourteen years built and maintained a successful tennis program. As a USPTA (United States Professional Tennis Association) Certified Instructor, she was involved in teaching as well as having management responsibility.

From a variety of jobs and a world of experience in human nature, Jan Hudgins was also at Buckhorn and found herself working with Mary as the office manager responsible for the tennis shop while providing racquet stringing for the players.

Due to the nature of a Country Club, they worked seven day weeks and twelve hour days. The morning players expected them for lessons and clinics during the day, and the evening and weekend players then expected lessons, tournaments, and socials in the evenings and on weekends. Holidays were a time for tennis parties. Relaxation for the members meant work for Mary and Jan. Although Mary loved teaching and playing tennis, the long hours year after year had their effect. For almost ten years she couldn't even participate in state or national tournaments as she was always at the "club."

Having worked together for eight years managing the tennis program, Mary and Jan felt they worked extremely well together but they were both ready for a career change. But what?

While brainstorming, Jan suggested a cleaning service and a club member who had gotten to be a close friend, encouraged them and even arranged a meeting with the office manager of her husbands real estate development company. With a commercial strip center and bank building as an account base, they suddenly found themselves in the cleaning business. Learning as they went, they acquired commercial cleaning equipment with the help of one of the local cleaning equipment suppliers and from on the job training (OJT) learned that dependability and honesty were the best selling tools.

Marketing consisted of letting their friends know they were in business and doing the best job they could for the accounts they had. Pricing was reasonable as they estimated the time it would take and had an hourly goal for themselves plus a small markup for cleaning supplies. They were soon making as much as they did at Buckhorn and working a lot fewer hours. They couldn't believe they had not gone into business for themselves sooner.

The loss of medical benefits and the security of a paycheck were replaced with having their days and weekends available for whatever they wanted. With only their accounts to take care of instead of every club member, a hundred problems a day suddenly became just a few. Mary began competing in state and national tennis tournaments and Jan continued stringing as a Certified Racquet Specialist through the United States Racquet Stringers Association.

Monday through Friday evening, however, were business days and if one couldn't work they developed a list of backups who were available so no account went unserviced and no children were allowed on the job. With just themselves and a few backup employees they ensured services were both dependable and thorough.

With this reputation and client referrals, they developed a base of customer accounts which kept them busy every evening. To maintain their reputation for dependability and quality service, if they didn't feel they could service an additional account properly they politely said they were just too busy at the present time. The intent was not to get rich or build a huge cleaning company with the same employee problems everyone else has, but to keep their overhead low and make a comfortable living.

Six years later, neither would have it any other way.

STARTING
A
HOME
BASED
BUSINESS

BALLOONIES, INC.

BALLOON DECORATIONS

Michele Harber was twenty nine, married, had a ten year old son, and hated working as a national sales assistant with a local television station. After nine years of clerical work in banking and only six months in her new job making $17,000 a year, Michele was fed up with long hours, low pay, and getting coffee. Anything, had to be better! One day, already on the verge of walking out without an option in mind, a delivery person brought in a balloon arrangement for her boss's birthday. Just one look at that balloon arrangement and she said to herself, "*I can do that!*" Michele turned in her two weeks notice that same day.

Armed with an ambition to be her own boss, a brand new clown suit, and a traveling helium tank **BALLOONIES** was born in October of 1984. With limited capital required, as helium tanks were $50.00 each, large "parade" type balloons cost $ .70 each, and a $99 clown suit, it was easy to get started. Loaded with balloons and an unlimited enthusiasm, it was $2.00 a balloon at every flea market, parade, or holiday crowd she could find. Every child was met with a smile, a hello, and "*What a beautiful child!*" How could a happy, honest, loving parent turn down a balloon!!!!

Selling one balloon at a time, however, was just the start. Although it was sure nice to end the day with a fistful of dollars and a lot of smiles, the business had to grow. The next transition was to a yellow page advertisement, flyers on every bulletin board in town, and a business card faster than a speeding bullet. Every night of the week was involvement in a community function. The Chamber of Commerce, Small Business Networking, the Head Start Program, etc. If you didn't know what to get for your anniversary or your wife's birthday, you knew Michele meant BALLOONIES, and a quick phone call meant a beautiful balloon arrangement delivered by a smiling clown.

The next thing you knew, was that a smiling clown would entertain at children's birthday parties with balloon animals, painted clown faces, and every child holding a helium filled balloon. If there were no birthday parties, it was Easter with a pink bunny rabbit delivering BALLOON-BASKETS to the children. If you weren't careful, and your wife knew you had forgotten your anniversary, on your birthday a life size gorilla would waltz into your office carrying a BALLOON ARRANGEMENT and singing happy birthday in front of all your friends.

Back on the homefront, at least Michele's husband and friends were a little more accepting than at the beginning. From *"You'll never make it."* and *"Please......get a real job,"* Michele's husband was now delivering balloon arrangements on weekends and occasionally the clown had a mustache or the gorilla had a real **deep** singing voice.

MARKETING DIRECTION

Although handing out business cards by the thousands, Michele had to keep the company growing as a $25-$35 balloon arrangement still had to be competitive with florists, who were also getting involved with balloons, and other home-based balloon competitors. Knowing the keys to success in this business were personal contacts and exposure, nobody was more enthusiastic, shook more hands, or passed out more business cards than BALLOONIES, Inc. But the question remained, "Where to grow the business next?"

There had to be a way to take the business from a limited volume, low dollar profit per arrangement, to higher profits per order. Although the profit in each arrangement was attractive since the materials cost for the balloons, ribbon, helium, etc. was nominal, the labor to make and deliver the arrangements limited the number of balloon arrangements which could be promised for a specific day.

The parties, however, were very profitable and provided an opportunity to leverage her own time by contracting some of the labor to part-time help. They also provided a larger potential billing so Michele decided to start directing her marketing towards corporate parties and wedding receptions as an alternative to traditional floral arrangements. In addition to being more cost effective, balloons also had the advantage of providing a vertical visual image with balloon columns and wedding arches. With an increased emphasis on flyers showing party themes, BALLOONIES had found a new direction.

In addition to corporate flyers, Michele was also displaying her balloon creations at Bridal Shows. She had a **BALLOONIES** booth and decorated the Bridal Show with balloons to allow the attendees to see the impact balloons can have on a large room. Michele then followed up every hopeful bride with a flyer and phone call based on the attendees list.

EVALUATION

From a financial standpoint, Michele indicated she was pleased with the progress of the company, especially the expansion into wedding receptions and corporate parties. Smiling, she also indicated the company was making more than she had ever made in a normal job.

After growing and working with the business for eight years, we also discussed the ups and downs of her own business. The most immediate concerns (which tend to be common in most small businesses) were:

1. Never having a day off as her busy times were weekends and holidays,
2. Always being in a marketing mode as success depended on personal contacts, and
3. Lack of family support and encouragement from her friends. *"I sometimes think they almost wanted me to fail."*

I asked if she ever thought she would go back to a normal job?   Michele started laughing.....and laughed.....and laughed! She was still laughing as I was leaving. Somehow, I don't think she will!

In retrospect, Michele took a tremendous risk in creating BALLOONIES with such limited preplanning. From a personal standpoint, her income was needed to help support a growing family as she had recently remarried. I asked, *"Did you think about what would happen if BALLOONIES didn't work out?"* Michele replied, *"I never let that thought enter my mind!"*

I wish I knew more people with as much courage and conviction.

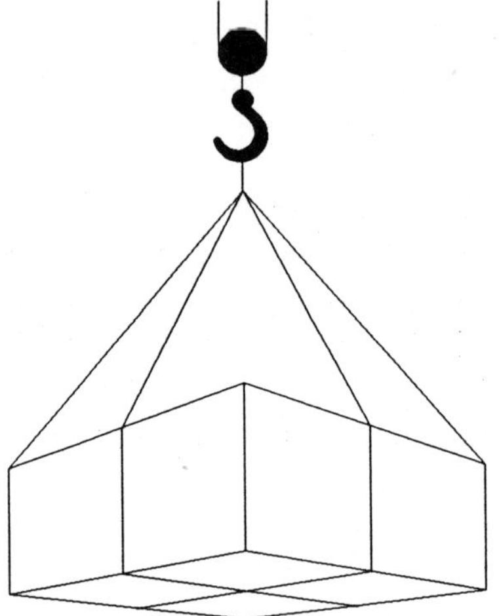

C & S CRANE SERVICE, INC.

MOBILE CRANE SERVICE

Bill Pinciotti grew up in the mobile crane business. From the time he could walk, driving an eighteen ton crane seemed as normal as driving a car. Growing up in Philadelphia, his father had a crane business with five mobile cranes. His uncle was in the crane business, also. It was natural that Bill and his brother started operating cranes in their father's company.

After three or four years of working for their father, Bill and his brother bought the crane business. *"Operating the cranes was easy,"* said Bill, *"but if two brothers could agree on something, we weren't able to find it."* Unable to work together, four years later, Bill and his brother sold the business to another crane company. They continued operating the cranes for the new company and Bill stayed with them for another ten years.

During the ten years, Bill continued to try building another company. With his brother-in-law, he started a furniture delivery business. Contracting with Levitz Furniture Stores, they began delivering customer purchases. Levitz scheduled the orders and retained 15% of the delivery charge, Bill's brother-in-law did the driving and delivered the furniture, while Bill took care of financing the delivery truck and the financial end of the business. His brother-in-law decided furniture delivery was not for him so it was time for a new business.

Bill's next adventure was a pressure washing business. This time with another brother. Bill purchased the truck and a high-pressure washer with all the necessary couplings and hoses for cleaning walls and roofs. Pressure washing was also a lot of work so his brother decided to try something else. For the second time, Bill was left with the equipment and no partner. Bill smiled as he said, *"Right then, I decided that was the last business venture with a relative."*

Tired of the long winters and seasonal slow down in construction work , Bill and his family began vacationing in Florida. It was not long before they decided that Florida looked awful nice as a year round residence. Mentioning the thought to his boss, the company suggested that if Bill was serious, they would send a mobile crane to Florida and have Bill start a Florida subsidiary. That offer was too good to turn down. At thirty-four, Bill, his wife Troy, and their three teenage children were headed for Florida.

With the crane loaded on a flatbed truck and on its' way south, Bill was soon in Tampa looking for business. Operating out of a home office he had an answering machine and mobile phone. Bill began calling on all the construction companies in the area.

MARKETING

Marketing was primarily a function of getting to know all the construction companies and home builders in the area. A crane service is not the type of business where the owner can send out brochures or advertise in trade journals. The construction foreman wants to know the crane operator and have confidence that the operator knows what he is doing. After eighteen years of operating cranes, Bill could use one to pour coffee during lunch.

Renting out the crane and operator by the hour, with a three hour minimum, Bill began offering the first rental with a company at half price in order to get to know the construction people. Although hesitant to use an operator they did not know, a normal job billed at $500-$600 for the day, offered at half price was too good to turn down. Bill began getting jobs and once the construction foreman had spent the day working with Bill, any operator concerns disappeared.

The mobile phone was critical as callers usually wanted a crane available the same day or the next day. His answering machine provided his mobile phone number and instructed the caller to call the mobile number if they needed to talk to Bill right away. The mobile phone became a permanent attachment to Bill as every business call was a potential job.

Mostly doing roof trusses for residential construction or second story or roof work for commercial buildings, construction was slow and many contractors were slow in paying their bills. To solve this problem, new accounts had to pay the day of the job, and ongoing accounts were provided an invoice at the job site, which the foreman had to sign. A copy was then sent to the construction office with payment due in thirty days. A few customers complained about the payment terms, but it is hard to lift the roof trusses on a house without a crane. No payment, no crane!

At the end of the first year, Bill felt pretty good about the accounts which he had established. The company in Philadelphia, however, felt they could earn more in Philadelphia due to the higher billing levels and union work so they moved the crane back north.

Bill, meanwhile, had been looking for a crane to purchase or an existing crane service to buy. Once you have spent the winter in Florida, it's difficult to go back north. He found a crane service for sale and purchased the business along with a 1975 eighteen ton crane with a 110ft. boom. *"I got really lucky,"* said Bill, *"I found a crane that would have cost $200,000 new and an owner-operator ready to retire just as I was looking to buy."*

By combining the new accounts with the ones that Bill had established during the past year, Bill is covering his expenses and crane payments during a very slow period in Florida construction. One of the keys to his success has been the overhead associated with a home-office. Bill does the billing, makes the sales calls, operates the crane, and even does the maintenance to keep his costs down. The savings allows him to offer a competitively priced crane service.

Most of his business is now repeat customers. Loyalty is important, but location and geography are also a consideration. Billing starts from the time Bill gets in the crane and ends when he parks the crane. Because the construction company is paying for transportation time, jobs tend to be within a limited geographical area. Having established himself in the area, Bill is positioned well to capitalize on any increase in construction activity.

I asked Bill about his long term plans for growth and found it interesting that Bill did not want to expand his crane service. As the single operator-owner of the crane service, Bill does not have to and does not want to worry about employees. In the construction business, employees are extremely unreliable. In addition, construction is extremely cyclical and in the good times multiple cranes are great, but when construction slows down who needs a couple of cranes with big loan payments sitting in storage.

EVALUATION

As a home based business, Bill is in an ideal position. With eighteen years of experience operating cranes and a significant investment to purchase a mobile crane, Bill does not have new competitors entering the business everyday. Having spent the last year and a half establishing a diverse customer base, Bill is positioned to benefit from increased construction. With a low overhead, more business means increased profits.

ANNOUNCEMENT
CORPORATE
LAYOFFS
2,000

D & B CREDIT CONSULTING, INC.

ACCOUNTS RECEIVABLE COLLECTIONS

With a twenty year career in credit and collections, Dennison Osborne operates D & B Credit Consulting, Inc. Working out of a home-based office, with an answering machine and an IBM compatible computer, he collects past due accounts receivable on a commission basis.

Dennison began his credit career in the early 1970's with Household Finance after finishing a tour with the U.S. Army. From Household he went on to Westinghouse Credit and then to a Real Estate Property Management Company as the Credit Manager for 16,000 rental units. Transferring to Florida in the mid 1980's, he was the Credit Manager for six years with the Olin Mott Tire Company.

In early 1990 he incorporated D & B Credit Consulting, Inc., with the thought of earning an extra income in his spare time and an eye on developing a home-based business which he could grow. In his late 40's, Dennison was ready to try something on his own.

"As the credit manager, I'm the whipping post for every salesman who can't close a deal and the company who wants sales at all costs. If I'm doing my job correctly it's a no win situation for me."

With a base salary and usually a small year end bonus, there is just no opportunity for upward growth in credit management unless you try something on your own. After a heated credit debate with management, he was finally ready to go full time with D & B Credit Consulting and left Olin Mott in September of 1990. After a full year on his own, like most beginning businesses, Dennison gained ten years experience in that one year period.

He originally thought companies would be willing to pay for a consultant to work with them in reviewing their credit practices, policies and collection procedures. Just the opposite has occurred, small companies haven't been willing to pay in advance to solve some of their future credit and collections problems, but they have been willing to pay a commission to collect past receivables which they have given up trying to collect. In some cases, they had even gotten

court judgements against the individuals, but the companies did not know how to convert the judgements to cash.

I probably seemed surprised that individuals would let past due balances go for years at a time and not expect the companies to initiate collection efforts. Retaining 50% of any collections on receivables outstanding for more than four months and 30% of any receivables less than four months old, I was amazed when he told me many of the receivables assigned to his company are three or four years old. "It's like they're testing me to see what kind of job I can do on the really old stuff." In most cases, Dennison explained that the companies are hesitant to aggressively pursue past due accounts as it is time consuming and most owners just do not want the emotional involvement and confrontations in trying to collect past due accounts.   In addition, considerable experience is required in searching court records to find any assets the individuals might own to attach, digging out checking or savings accounts which they have, or in going to the effort of garnishing their wages.

Collecting does not have to be an emotional confrontation, but the job has to be approached with persistance and a business attitude. It's not always pleasant, but on the other hand, it's just not fair to the business owners providing a service and trying to make a living to let the past due accounts just walk away. In some cases it's a problem with financial conditions which have overwhelmed a person and he tries to work out a settlement or a repayment schedule. In other cases the past due amount is in dispute and Dennison ends up as an arbitrator trying to work out an equitable settlement. Once in a while, however, the creditor has no intent to pay. They have probably gotten away with not paying in the past and do not expect the company to aggressively pursue their past due account. In these cases, Dennison doesn't hesitate to attach assets or get a garnishment.

MARKETING

When Dennison first started his business, he placed classified advertisements in the local newspaper and didn't receive a single call. From there, he began personally calling on other tire companies since he had been in the tire business for the past six years. The personal calls got results as the collection efforts were on a commission basis. If he did not perform, there was no charge. He even made it a point to personally deliver the check for those past due accounts which he was able to collect. *"I wanted to personally reinforce the immediate cash benefit to the company of working with me."* For the most part, these were accounts the companies had already written off and never expected to see a dime.

The second step was to begin networking with other small businesses who had collection problems. Of course, every small business had accounts receivable, so Dennison joined the local Chamber of Commerce to get to know the members. He then expanded his personal calls to prior business relationships. A polite way of saying he began to offer his collection services to companies he had collected past due receivables from. He reasoned, if they did not have collection problems themselves, they would not have had problems paying their own bills. Dennison had handled their past due problems in a professional manner and a number of the companies responded by having D & B Credit handle their own outstanding receivables.

Recognizing many people did not know how to collect judgements, Dennison next searched the Hillsborough County Courthouse records to identify judgements which had been recorded against properties. Writing a letter to the judgement owners, Dennison offered to provide collection services based on finding other assets which could be levied or through garnishing their wages. A number of those letters also provided collection opportunities.

In summarizing his accounts, all the leads were due to personal sales calls or referrals. General advertising did not produce a single lead.

As he reviewed the past year, he feels discipline is the key to any home-based business. It's so easy to get distracted and not make the collection calls or send out the letters or do the courthouse research. The potential, however, is there for anyone willing to work hard at their business. Being home-based simply reduces the overhead expenses and provides a greater chance for success. When I asked if he thought he could go back to a normal job environment, Dennison smiled, looked around his home and said, *"I don't think I could."*

THE FLYER SERVICE

REALTOR FLYER DELIVERY SERVICE

Lori Reeves is on the run every minute coordinating and delivering flyers and newsletters to real estate offices located in three counties. With an incredibly simple idea and an equally promising future, you think to yourself, *"Why didn't I come up with that idea?"*

In her early forties, Lori found herself with two children, a home to sell, an ex-husband, and $500 in the bank. Married after high school in the 1960's, she had been a homemaker raising her children, taking care of the house, and working an occasional part time job to help with extras. *"The last thing in the world I wanted,"* she said, *"was to be running a full time business."*

Working part time as a receptionist in a real estate firm, her immediate concern was, *"What do I do now?"* As she thought about her options, she watched individual real estate associates prepare flyers on current real estate listings, get in their cars, and deliver the flyers to every real estate office in the area. As soon as one salesperson would leave, another would be on the copier making flyers for a commercial listing, or an open  house this Sunday, or a change in price and owner financing on a currently listed home. It was a constant parade of cars driving the exact same route each delivering their flyers.

As she started to visualize the duplication of the delivery effort, she realized how often new businesses and companies supporting the real estate industry dropped off flyers to the office for her to distribute to the real estate associates. It might be a flyer from a mortgage company listing the latest interest rates, terms and points (prepaid interest) required, or a local builder providing a weekly inventory sheet with revised prices, homes that had sold, special features, financing packages available, or special sales contest prizes and incentives. Even the local dry cleaner and a bakery dropped off "special discount coupons" for families moving into the area.

It seemed everyone with a local product or service wanted the real estate associates to know about it because they were the first contact with families moving into a new area. For months after buying and moving into a new home, the newcomers would call up and ask, *"We are looking for .... and wondered if you could provide a referral?"* It was like the local real estate office was a permanent welcome wagon for every new resident.

Because Lori was only working part time as the receptionist, she began offering to deliver the flyers to the brokerage offices for the associates in her office. Pretty soon, Lori was scheduling her delivery trips and delivering flyers for several associates on one trip. Suddenly the trips became worthwhile as each associate paid to have their flyers delivered while Lori only incurred the cost of one trip. Realizing this idea would give her some time to sell her home and decide what to do with her life, Lori paid $200 to rent a desk for a month at the real estate office and she was in business.

Everything in this book about personal and business planning, marketing, accounting, and corporate structures occasionally can be forgotten. Sometimes personal circumstances dictate an action plan and not being successful is simply not an alternative. With an incredible enthusiasm and personality that is always smiling, Lori soon had an established delivery route to every real estate office in the area and was delivering flyers for associates in every office. Not only did she deliver flyers to each office but she picked up flyers to be delivered to other offices. In no time at all, Lori ceased to exist, as she entered each office with a smile it was simply, *"The Flyer Lady is here."*

With all of her business coming from referrals, Lori kept her costs low and she soon had her hands full with the builders and real estate associates providing the majority of her steady customers. Outgrowing a single desk at the real estate office, she quickly moved her business into her home with a dining room table for collating flyers, a living room with space for a computer and printer for billing and preparing an occasional flyer, a copier to make flyers for her clients and a large desk. Delivering flyers at a considerable savings over the post office, Lori also provided a personalized touch as she would place a flyer in the inbox for each sales associate or simply provide a single office copy if desired by her clients. With each real estate office getting to know her as she delivered on a regular scheduled route, they saw her on the same day each week. The personalized delivery service put many of the flyers in the hands of the associates instead of a company receptionist simply filing flyers delivered through the mail in the "round file next to the desk" along with the rest of the junk mail.

EVALUATION

Five years later, Lori is in the process of establishing real estate office routes in the surrounding counties. Beginning initially with approximately 175 real estate offices and around 1700 real estate associates in the immediate county, the three county area should provide plenty of long term growth. Still working out of her home, Lori has finally recognized the need to expand her service with additional drivers as she establishes the new routes. Her drivers, of course, being new home-based businesses.

She is also expanding the preparation of flyers for businesses. With an Apple computer, Lori is starting to do layout and design for customer flyers. Lori just had 5,000 flyers printed for her own business and deliverd them along with her other flyer deliveries. *"I've gotten so many calls I am tired of answering the phone,"* she said.

Sitting there talking with Lori was a pleasure. The delivery possibilities seemed endless. Every small business providing a product or service on a local basis is an ideal candidate to send flyers to the local real estate offices. Even a small business with a limited advertising budget can still afford the cost of printing and delivering flyers as it is one of the most cost effective methods of advertising available. In addition, flyers seem to be a very effective method as they are timely and can be delivered on a regular basis. For example, in most cases, flyers are picked up for delivery throughout the week and almost without exception, every flyer is delivered by Monday of the following week. Getting the flyers delivered by Monday provides the real estate associates with the latest information. Saturdays and Sundays are usually just another work day getting the flyers collated and sometimes making deliveries if Monday looks like a busy day.

Overall the combination of a cost effective advertising medium and delivery schedule to put the information in the hands of the associates has proven to be a successful formula. Lori still says, *"I never wanted to be in business or to run a business."* Somehow, I think it's too late to turn back the clock now.

FREEDOM
INDEPENDENCE

GLOBE-CON INTERNATIONAL, INC.

THE GLOBAL FASTENER CONNECTION

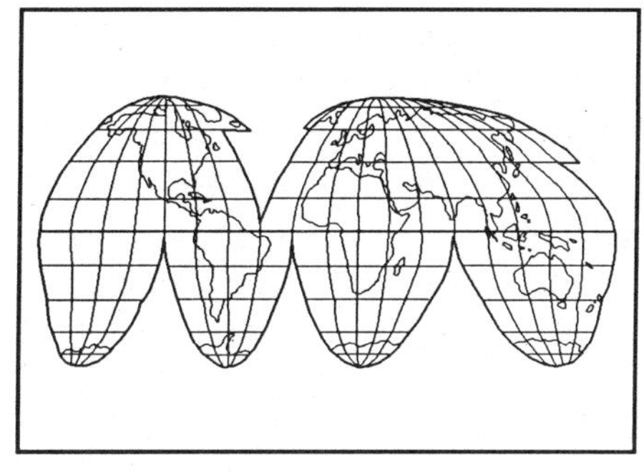

At thirty-eight, Frank Bordas and his wife, Sue, were ready to live life on their own terms. Just two years after being transferred to New Jersey as Vice President of Sales they were tired of the congestion, high cost of living, commuting, and the winters just kept getting longer. While vacationing in Florida and enjoying the perfect weather, he thought *"Why can't every day be like this?"* That was it! They had been vacationing on the west coast of Florida for the previous ten years and that is were they were headed.

Frank had spent the last eighteen years living and working on Long Island in New York. After a year of college, he started working in the warehouse of a wholesale fastener distribution company which stocked and distributed bolts, nuts, and metal screws throughout the United States. With ambition and hard work, Frank was soon in the office doing inside sales, accounting and starting to learn the purchasing end of the business. From the office, he was soon doing outside sales calling on manufacturing plants throughout the Southeastern United States. Sales success led to starting up a metric sales division for another Long Island company which had primarily been involved in wholesaling standard U.S. threaded nuts, bolts, and metal screws.

With responsibility for metric sales and purchasing, Frank began to develop an international expertise in importing and contracting as the metric suppliers were primarily foreign manufacturing plants in Japan, South Korea, and Taiwan. Making several trips to the Orient per year to meet the manufacturing representatives and order metal screws, nuts and bolts by the ton, Frank learned the international side of the business. He had to price and contract for international insurance, shipping, customs, duties, and port of entry requirements as he arranged for import to the U.S.

In addition to operating a direct shipment program where the orders were shipped directly from the factory to the customer, the company also operated a warehouse program where they purchased and imported the nuts and bolts, stored them, and then wholesaled smaller quantities. With a profit margin in the area of 10-15% on the direct shipment orders and 25%-30% on the warehouse operation, it was an interesting and profitable business.

Finally progressing to Vice President of Sales with responsibility for both metric and standard, as well as direct shipment and the warehouse operation, there wasn't much Frank did not know about the business from import all the way to the primary customers in the industry. The job and company could not have been better until the corporation moved to New Jersey. Instead of the rural atmosphere and lifelong friends in Long Island, they were in the heart of the New York City to Newark, New Jersey industrial metropolitan area. An area where housing costs and property taxes doubled, and mortgage payments were gigantic just to get a reasonable house. This was a community with a BMW or Mercedes in every garage and limousines delivering the neighbors' children to elementary school. With long hours at work and a declining economy putting a lot of pressure on the company, life was just not as much fun as it had been.

Florida started looking better every day...........! The house went up for sale and Frank agreed to establish and operate a Tampa, Florida based distribution warehouse for another wholesale importer. With the home about to close and having already resigned from his old position, Frank had second thoughts about the new company and decided not to start with them. But, he was still going to Florida.

With his home sale closed and capital in the bank to provide financial security for two to three years, Frank felt comfortable in making the move. A chance meeting with one of his customers however, provided the foundation for GLOBE-CON INTERNATIONAL, INC. and the opportunity to start his own company. Operating out of a home-based office to minimize the overhead, Frank realized that he had the international contacts and expertise to order and import nut, bolts, and screws. He began to contract directly with a few of his old customers to import their fastener needs with the nuts, bolts, and screws shipped directly to the customer location.

Frank was doing exactly what he had been doing for the last ten years for someone else. Only now, it was his business and his office which just happened to be in his home. With two business telephone lines and a fax machine to send and receive contracts, he was in business. The only other office equipment he used was a typewriter to prepare shipping orders and invoices.

His customers didn't know and didn't care where his office was and the manufacturing plants in the Orient certainly didn't care as long as the orders came in and the customers' checks cleared. There was certainly no need to tell them the white shirt, silk tie, and wool three piece suit had been replaced by sun glasses, tennis shorts, and an "open collar" knit shirt.

With almost no overhead, the markup on the orders could be considerably less than charged by the existing major importers. With this approach in mind, Frank was able to negotiate a contract with a major customer at about half the going profit margin in exchange for a guaranteed minimum volume of business for the year. With this guarantee providing a financial base for his business, Frank began attending trade association meetings to promote his business. These association expenses along with a couple of trips to the Orient each year to develop new manufacturing contacts and renew existing relationships are the only significant expenses incurred. The only ongoing overhead expense other than general office supplies is the telephone bill due to the volume of international faxes confirming and following up orders.

EVALUATION

Frank is taking the most opportune approach to working on his own. He is doing exactly what he has been doing for the past ten years. The only things Frank changed were the name of the company, his business location, and he added a little mental insecurity since he doesn't have a whole company to support him.

On the other hand, instead of a salary and bonus, Frank is in a position to substantially increase his income since his import fee is based on the size of order as a percentage of the cost. From an administrative standpoint, it takes exactly the same level of work to import a $25,000 order with a 6% markup as a $250,000 order with the same 6% markup. In fact, as the orders get larger, he can even reduce the percentage of markup and be more competitive while increasing his overall income.

The key to his success, will be Frank's ability to monitor and follow up the orders with an administrative system to ensure the orders get delivered, invoiced, and collected. This administrative side has always been taken care of by an administrative staff, but now Frank and his wife are the administrative staff.

From a marketing standpoint, the wholesale fastener industry is pretty well defined so the potential market is very specific. This means that marketing is primarily one on one through personal sales calls and attendance at trade shows and is based on building a personal relationship as opposed to lots of advertising and mass marketing. Frank does plan on developing a company brochure, but it is really just a way to add credibility to his business as potential customers ask for a proposal or specific quote on an order.

Having just purchased a home, pool and jacuzzi included, Frank and Sue are committed to a Florida lifestyle. After having a home-based business of his own for just a year, I asked him if the opportunity presented itself would he consider working as an executive in a corporate environment again? He thought about it for a few seconds and said, *"Not if I can help it!"*

THE "ME" KIT STORY

PERSONAL GROWTH WORKSHOPS

"On November 19, 1986. My boss called me to a 1:30 meeting. He began, I don't know how to tell you this, Gordon, but you are being laid off....and we would like you to leave by 4:30, because if you're still here at 5:00 when everyone else leaves, it'll be depressing." This is the way Gordon Hill introduces his personal growth workshops.

An Electrical Engineer by training from the University of Missouri, Gordon Hill, for the third time in a thirty year corporate career was looking for a job. This time was different though. When you are thirty with a decade of experience in General Motors, the whole world lies ahead and changing companies is an opportunity for advancement and career growth. At forty, after a decade in computer sales and technical support, the horizon does not seem so far away and the sun is not as bright. At fifty, settled in corporate technical marketing support with an electronics manufacturer, being laid off with limited hope the company is going to get back on its' feet, is a serious challenge.

After breakfast with a friend, Gordon decided to start his own company. As his friend summed up the situation, *"If you start your own business, you'll never be fired and you'll never get laid off."* There is absolutely no question about the truthfulness of that observation. But after a thirty year career in large corporations, just how do you go about starting a new business. And more importantly want do you do? What kind of business? How do you market yourself?

With corporate America downsizing, these questions have almost universal application as many midcareer professionals are finding themselves facing the same questions. Too young to retire and too old to start a career with another company. Do they stay in the same basic career specialization or do they get into an entirely new field? In Gordon's case, he decided to build on his existing professional expertise and corporate experience in teaching technical seminars and workshops. Utilizing those exact skills, he decided to conduct corporate training workshops and seminars in electronic data and voice communications as a consultant.

With a financial commitment set aside to last a year, he provided a specific planning horizon to evaluate the performance of his company and determine if he should continue in corporate training.   Initially conducting communications workshops on a contract basis for an existing technical training firm, marketing was not a problem. Long term success, however, depended upon Gordon developing his own course material and marketing his own workshops. Teaching on a contract basis paid the overhead, but the real money went to the company.

Gordon is active in the National Speakers Association, on both a local and national basis, in order to improve his verbal communication and workshop leadership skills.   He spends the balance of his time developing technical training materials for his own courses, writing, and in telemarketing to major corporations. Working out of a home office with an IBM compatible computer and laser printer, the workshop materials and page diagrams appear very professional.   Utilizing wordprocessing software and a graphics program, Gordon's technical background is clearly evident.

At the end of his first year evaluation period, Gordon decided to continue developing his business. In fact, although his workshops and training seminars have taken a different turn, Gordon is still in business and it has been five years. During the last few years as corporations have lowered their training budgets as a result of the general economic recession, as well as a shift in the direction of Gordon's personal interests, he has been conducting fewer and fewer multi-day corporate communications workshops. Instead, he has been focusing his attention on workshops and presentations on personal growth utilizing a concept called the "ME" Kit which he developed.

Gordon's personal growth programs range from a thirty minute after-dinner speech called Your Magnificent "ME" Kit, to an hour workshop entitled Becoming Ourselves, a half day program Trading Up Using Your "ME" Kit, or a full day retreat called Who I Am Not/Who I Am/Who I Can Be.

In conjunction with his workshops, Gordon has been writing about personal growth in an effort to expand his marketing and professional recognition. His initial effort has been the first in a series of personal growth columns which he plans to write and publish on a weekly basis. In addition to submitting each column to local newspapers for publication, Gordon plans to use the personal growth articles in his direct mail marketing.

EVALUATION

Just by surviving five years in a very tough business, Gordon has shown an intense determination to succeed. Corporate training as a consultant is difficult, at best, unless you are teaching a very specific technical seminar which is generally unavailable within the corporation. This is due to the cost of external trainers and an emphasis on moving as much training to inhouse corporate instructors as possible.

Gordon's shift to Personal Growth Workshops is also a difficult transition, especially in a recessionary period, due to the generalized nature and long term benefit of the workshops. In today's economic environment, corporations are looking for a specific, direct link between an investment in training and an increase in job performance. Personal Growth Workshops are wonderful, but they are a discretionary expense which can be deferred when the economy is lean.

Given the personal nature of the business, Gordon has focused his primary marketing emphasis on direct telemarketing to corporations in the area. Using a directory of corporations, Gordon simply calls and asks for the person responsible for corporate training. Most every company will provide the individual in the training or human resources department who has training responsibility. From there, it is all salesmanship. He does follow up with marketing literature and has a demonstration cassette tape which is available.

The key to marketing in this industry, however, is public exposure and referrals from existing speaking engagements. What I mean by this statement, is that your best lead is one generated by someone who has heard your presentation. Telemarketing will only get your foot in the door but the product, your workshop, is difficult to sell because it has been difficult to show exactly what the workshop is.

The best exposure is to perform as many speaking engagements to civic and professional organizations as possible even though they are lunch or dinner meetings and the mini-workshops are free. The audience, however, contains potential clients which can provide referrals or hopefully provide an entre' to the company they work for. They are the best leads because they have heard a part of your workshops and can measure your effectiveness.

MORE THAN SURVIVAL

TRAINING WORKSHOPS & SEMINARS

At 41, Sheryl Nicholson has her days full balancing **MORE THAN SURVIVAL** a successful corporate training firm, four older children, a husband, a beautiful home, and a seven day old infant.

After seven years of workshop development, marketing, and teaching corporate seminars in self esteem, communications, problem solving skills, customer service, and goal setting, Sheryl thought she was finally ready to slow down. With the two older children on their own, it was time to enjoy her family and continue growing her company. Life is not so simple, a just born baby girl, unwanted, about to be placed in a HRS foster home, reached out and grabbed her heart. "How could I let this beautiful little girl go into a HRS foster home?"

Life has not always been so good. Married at 19 to a college student from Sweden, Sheryl spent the next three years in Sweden raising her two new babies and supporting her husband while he worked on a doctoral program before the family returned to the United States. A second husband, two more children, a real estate license, and in her mid thirties, Sheryl was tired of "raising husbands" as well as children.

With a background in real estate sales and sales training, Sheryl had been selling and scheduling real estate training and motivational seminars for Steven Oniki, a well known sales trainer. Ready to end her second marriage, Sheryl moved to Miami to manage a Real Estate School for a local broker. On her own again, with four children to support and limited financial savings, Sheryl knew she could make it. A month later, the Real Estate School closed down due to the death of the owner.

Back in Tampa, during the process of a year and a half divorce, Sheryl ended up in corporate sales for Dale Carnegie Seminars. Calling on corporate clients to enroll management employees in the three Dale Carnegie courses (1) Effective Speaking

And Human Relations, (2) Salesmanship, and (3) Management Skills, Sheryl was the top salesperson for two years.   While calling on corporate management and giving seminar previews to potential corporate sponsors, Sheryl found herself limited in her own career advancement as she could not progress into teaching Dale Carnegie Courses without a college degree.   At $25,000 a year, she was bubbling with enthusiasm, had a lifetime of human relations experience to share, and was tired of "other" people controlling her life, saying **NO**, and telling her what she could and could not do!

She says, "*I was ready to explore my own limits.*" With her last paycheck for the year in hand and the Christmas holidays about to start, Sheryl decided to start the new year with her own corporate training company.   After selling management personnel Dale Carnegie Courses at $800 each, she realized there was a tremendous opportunity to teach corporate training workshops and seminars for the administrative and corporate support staffs who where generally ignored.   With the majority of training dollars allocated to management, little remained for the balance of the company employees especially in the smaller companies with no internal training departments.

There was a need for human relations training which could be provided on an economical basis at the corporate location, with the corporation providing the training room, at a fixed seminar rate irrespective of the number of atteendees. By maximizing the number of administrative participants, the cost or investment in each participant becomes nominal. Maybe the company is not willing to invest in a $800 Dale Carnegie Course for each employee, but a $800 inhouse workshop divided by ten participants is only $80 each, or twenty participants only $40 each.

Armed with a business card and course proposal, Sheryl started the year calling on the corporate clients which she had already gotten to know. Seven years and countless seminars later, Sheryl is still at it. Armed with a fax machine and mobile phone with call forwarding on her business line she is still making sales calls. The selling and marketing process never ends. The seven years have seen lots of ups and downs with countless free presentations in getting started and establishing her reputation. Every civic club in the area wants you to speak, "*Think of the great exposure,*" they always say. It is true, the exposure to the business community is excellent, but at some point it is nice to receive a check along with a handshake.

From a $100 honorarium for speaking, Sheryl's client list has grown to include companies like IBM Corporation, Honeywell, Aetna Life Insurance, Ford, AT&T, and Anheuser Busch. Her fees have also grown to $750 for a keynote speech, $1,000 for a half day workshop, $2,000 for a full day program, or $3,600 for a six week Workshop Series. The Series consists of six one hour weekly workshops, a needs assessment to tailor the program to the company, weekly assignments, and followup to assess the effectiveness of the training.

Growth has not come easy, but working out of her home has reduced the overhead to almost nothing. A phone bill, typesetting and printing charges for her Seminar Manuals and promotional flyers are her primary expenses. Any other charges are for miscellaneous office supplies. Her next purchase, however, will be a lazer jet printer and computer to replace the typesetting and printing which she currently has done for her.

MARKETING

Although Sheryl uses promotional brochures and tapes of her seminars for marketing, the primary source of new business is still referral or personal contact. The key to success is getting in front of as many people as you can. Every speech has the potential to generate additional workshops and seminars from the existing audience. Companies tend to call someone for training whom they already know. Therefore, get in front of as many trade associations, professional organizations, civic groups, or dinner meetings as you can. Although, unpaid, view the speaking engagement as the cost of marketing, kind of like Amos's Chocolate Cookies standing in a shopping mall handing out free cookies to the shoppers. You have got to wet their appetite to get their attention.

As her next step in advertising and promotion, Sheryl wrote and published a book, *WORKING WOMEN ARE WORKING WONDERS* which she sells along with her seminars and workshops. In addition to providing the sales revenue, the book sales are also a potential lead to future seminar business. Although specifically oriented to working women the book has also enhanced her business reputation in corporate training seminars due to her appearance on several local television talk shows. With the future in mind, *"motivational cassette tapes are next,"* she says.

EVALUATION

Since Sheryl has been teaching training workshops and seminars, she has had lots of opportunities to go back to work full time with different clients. A few years back, one sounded too good to pass up. Sales and Training Manager for a Real Estate Development & Sales Company, salary and bonus of $60,000 a year plus free housing and a company car. It sounded so good, she accepted, and moved her family about 30 miles into one of the development homes. Six months later the company reorganized and eliminated her position...! Security is what you make for yourself.

She moved to her present home which she purchased. Sheryl started making calls to conduct training workshops and decided right then, *"That is the last time I ever work for anybody again."*

PARADISE VENDING

SNACKS, SODA, & CANDY VENDING

If it's broke or you need one, at fifty five, Merrill Nipper can fix it, design it, build it, install it, and monitor it.

Merrill started his career with a degree in Industrial Instrumentation from Polk Community College in Winter Haven, Florida. From there he worked fourteen years with Tampa Electric Company maintaining, engineering, building, and installing instrumentation to monitor and control equipment throughout the company. Along with a fellow employee, he left Tampa Electric to work as a consultant on a contract basis with the Industrial Instruments Division of Combustion Engineering, a company with international holdings.

Starting with a consulting base in the Southeastern United States, he was soon traveling internationally. With consulting assignments ranging from small instrument design to a five year contract with Agrico Chemical Company to design, build, and install all the industrial instruments in an entire phosphate processing plant, Merrill, didn't know from one week to the next where he might be.

The consulting relationship changed in 1974, however, as Combustion Engineering reassessed their corporate strategic plans and decided to sell the Industrial Instruments Division. Merrill and a partner suddenly found themselves borrowing all they could from a local bank, and renting a warehouse in Tampa. Putting on his company hat as the President, Merrill was trying to figure out what to do with semi-truck loads of equipment, instruments, panels, and spare parts on their way to Tampa from Combustion Engineering.

Fourteen years later, at age 52, Merrill decided it was time to begin thinking about retirement, or at least semi-retirement. Accepting a buy-out offer from his partner, Merrill was too young to completely retire and way too "old" to think about a job. With most of his retirement savings tied up in a corporate pension (401K tax deferred compensation plan), he did not want to begin drawing on his retirement savings to avoid any potential IRS penalty for early withdrawal.

It was time to start a part time business out of his home to keep himself busy and provide an income for the next four or five years. After several months of looking and evaluating, Merrill started PARADISE VENDING to market soft drinks, candy, and snack foods. Initially purchasing an existing vending company with twenty-one vending machines installed at different locations, it was not long before he began adding new machines as customers requested additional services such as coffee and soup machines, food vending, or needed larger capacity soft drink machines holding 501 cans instead of 368. With the purchase of another "twenty vending machine" company and still more new machines, Merrill was soon chest deep in potato chips, cookies, candy bars, sandwiches, and cases of soda pop as he was trying to service eighty-one "always empty" machines. In just three years, Merrill had grown his home-based business right out of his home.

Starting with his office and inventory in the smallest bedroom of his home, as the children were adults and on their own, he was soon in the largest bedroom, until finally his wife, Faye kicked him out to the "barn."

Not a normal "barn " but one designed and built by Merrill to accommodate the airconditioned storage of the vending inventory, his office, room to repair all the vending machines, space for his machine tools, and an extra room to restore and paint antique cars in his spare time. Just to make it more of a challenge, he even designed and built a compressed air system with outlets throughout the rooms to plug his compressed air powered tools and paint sprayer into. There was even covered parking for four automobiles and a stall attached to the end for his horse.

Whoever thought semi-retirement meant you were supposed to semi-retire clearly did not know Merrill. With Faye and his son-in-law also working full time for PARADISE VENDING, the business was getting to be a full time job. Merrill was handling all the vending machine repairs, most of the purchasing, keeping a personal computer based inventory program up to date, preparing monthly financial statements, and figuring out how to finance the growing inventory and number of vending machines. With a cost in the range of $2,200 to $2,700 each, new machines required a significant outlay of capital.

Faye and their son-in-law were out each day loading the machines and collecting the change. With the number of machines, loose change to you and I, required the purchase of coin and dollar bill counting machines and daily trips to the bank. Commissions and sales tax had to be calculated on each machine and paid monthly. Sales tax went to the Florida State Sales Tax Division and a location commission of around 10% was paid monthly to the companies where the machines were located.

With rust on his golf clubs and even new Nike's unable to help his tennis game, it was time to get serious about semi-retirement. Realizing the older smaller vending machines were taking up a disproportionate amount of time to service and maintain, Merrill sold a route of 13 older machines to another vending company wanting to expand. With one eye on retirement in a few years, he also sold part of the business to his son-in-law with plans to sell him the remaining business over the next few years. With the "barn" almost done and a 1940 Buick along with a 1941 Chevrolet ready to restore there just was not enough time in the day.

EVALUATION

Merrill has done a tremendous job in building PARADISE VENDING into a successful home-based business, but the challenges and skills required are different than most other home-based businesses. Instead of marketing, which is usually the biggest challenge in most small businesses, a vending machine company requires the ability to finance the investment capital required to purchase the machines and is relatively labor intensive.

The labor is a combination of skilled and unskilled in the sense that the servicing of the vending route (keeping the machines stocked) can be done by anyone with a truck and reasonable driving record (automobile liability insurance based on commercial usage is expensive). The office functions of purchasing and record keeping are also fairly easy. Accurate record keeping, however, is one of the keys to a successful company as the vending machine sales are constantly monitored and the machines moved to different locations if the sales are not profitable. Different locations also have unique profiles with respect to machine abuse and theft.

Vending machine maintenance requires skilled and reasonably expensive labor to maintain the equipment as it begins to wear. In addition, if the machines are older, parts often have to be rebuilt or redesigned as they may be unavailable or need to be ordered from the factory which may require a substantial waiting period.   If maintenance and repairs are contracted through the distributer or service companies, the hourly repair charges have a severe impact on your profitability. To be successful, I would suspect that the owners have to be in a position and have the available space to maintain the machines themselves or have a base of machines and the sales revenue to support a full time maintenance person.

The second unique challenge is the financing of the vending machines.   Using an average cost of $2,500 a machine, it is immediately apparent that a significant investment is required to expand the business. Bank borrowing while trying to start a vending business based on the cost of the vending machines is probably limited due to the nature of the collateral. I doubt the banks place much emphasis on the vending machines themselves, but look more to the financial strength of the individual. Given the size of the loan, you're probably looking at a secured loan based on a second mortgage or line of credit on your home. Another alternative would be financing through the vending machine manufacturer or if purchased from an individual or existing vending company, getting the seller to finance the purchase.

DONALD B. PATE, P.A.

INCOME TAX & ACCOUNTING SERVICES

About to turn forty, an accountant with the same company for the last eleven years, and settled in a beautiful custom built home he and his wife had designed, the last thing Don expected was to be unemployed again.

Growing up in a modest Tampa neighborhood in the early 1950's, Don decided that accounting was a good way to make a living, while watching his self-employed father working on the family business. Accountants worked indoors, wore clean shirts, and had a nice desk with lots of fancy looking equipment! Working during the day and bicycling each evening to Tampa College to save money for tuition he finally got his two year degree in accounting.

His first "real" job was with a local CPA and lasted for a year before getting hired away as the "bookkeeper" by one of their clients. As a way to earn a little extra he soon started doing personal income tax returns. Just like a family doctor, Don made house calls preparing the tax return in the clients' home. He still remembers taking the bus to his first client's home and charging her $4 for the tax return.

The next ten years were a succession of working for small companies, as they stayed in business a few years and then closed. They all needed accountants but there did not seem to be much security. Continuing to build his evening income tax practice, Don still made house calls as a convenience to his clients and the referrals kept the business growing. Approaching forty, an accountant for the last eleven years with a local machine and welding company servicing the shrimp boats working the Gulf of Mexico, the last thing Don expected was the company to begin failing. As the shrimp industry felt the recession in the early 1970's so went the machine shop.

Knowing his job was about to end, Don decided he was finished working for someone else. If he went out of business at least it was his own failure and he did not have to depend on anyone else. He began offering accounting and tax preparation services on a full time basis working out of his home. With his wife working for the County and providing medical insurance and a financial safety net, the financial downside was limited. If he could not get enough business, he would just be looking for a job again.

Using an adding machine and a typewriter, Don began expanding his business with client referrals and personal contacts. With a firm belief in professional development as well as community service, Don was active in the Florida Association of Independent Accountants, the local Chamber of Commerce, and the Kiwanis (a civic association).   The Florida Association of Independent Accountants (FAIA) provided an opportunity to associate with other accounting professionals as well as continuing professional education through tax seminars and workshops.   Along the way, Don also finished a four year degree in Accounting and became an Enrolled Agent based on passing a two day examination administered by the Treasury Department.   As an Enrolled Agent, Don has the right to represent a taxpayer in tax matters with the Internal Revenue Service the same as Certified Public Accountants (CPA's) and attorneys.   In the FAIA, Don has gone on to serve as an officer of the local chapter as well as on boards and committees of both the state and national associations.

In the local Chamber of Commerce he has held a term on the Board of Directors and served on numerous committees.   With advertising limited to a display advertisement in the phone book and an occasional coupon in a local advertising flyer, Don feels the only way to provide growth in a personal service business is through personal referrals from his existing clients and personal contacts.

"If you're thinking about a personal service business, get active in as many professional and civic associations as you can. Don't expect phone calls the first day you shake their hand, but if you're hardworking, competent, and get to know the other members they'll start sending referrals and even stop by if they need your services," said Don.

After eight years of building a client base, Don was preparing about 300 tax returns a year and monthly financial statements for about twenty small businesses. Don was still using an adding machine and typewriter, as personal computers were just starting to become available although not very affordable in the early 1980's. He had retired the green eye shade however.

Don was now facing his first major crisis. Although still making house calls for some of his long term clients, Don had shifted most of his client contact to his home due to the number of returns he was preparing. Unlike a normal office environment, however, most of his client meetings were in the evening and clients often had a different perception of a home-based business as opposed to a normal office based business. Somehow the home environment creates a sense of informality which does not normally exist in an office setting. Rachel would come home from a hectic day at work ready to relax and have a nice quiet dinner to find four strange children camped out in her family room watching television or playing with her crystal collection. It was always, *"My wife had to run some errands, so I hope you don't mind my children watching television while we work on my tax return?"*

Rachel was fed up with babysitting children. It was her home and she did not intend to come home during the four month tax season and find clients, especially ones she did not even know, camped out in her family room. Something had to change. Now!

Don had a couple of choices. He could tell his clients they could not bring their wives or children over, but how could he tactfully say that and keep his clients? He could reduce his client list to continue providing accounting services to his monthly accounts and the more expensive individual tax returns. Like most businesses 80% of his revenue probably came from 20% of his clients. The last alternative was to move the business out of his home and into a "real" office. No television and no babysitting services available.

COMMERCIAL OFFICE SPACE

Although reluctant, a commercial office seemed the most viable alternative as Don had simply outgrown his home-based office. Don leased space in a brand new commercial strip center with approximately eight other offices each approximately 900 square feet of unfinished space. The unfinished space meant leasehold improvements including interior walls, carpeting, wallpaper, and custom designed furniture.

With an office, he needed a new telephone system, and of course, a conference room without furniture looks a little barren. In fact, clients expect a normal accounting office to have a full time receptionist so Rachel soon quit her full time job and began working as the office manager for the accounting firm. From zero overhead a month, Don probably went to $3,000 a month including the loss of Rachel's salary and a significant investment in new furniture and leasehold improvements. The office, however, was first class.

The practice continued growing and soon Don began adding office help to operate the two new computers as he began computerizing the monthly accounting clients. He resisted, but tax preparation software also followed in a few years. Don soon faced his second major crisis. During his third tax season in the new office Don got ill and required hospitalization. He suddenly realized that the office staff was primarily clerical support and the accounting and tax service which he provided were 100% dependent on his personal involvement and knowledge. With Rachel also in the office, he realized their total livelihood depended on the success and income of the accounting practice.

It had not been as serious when he first started, when Rachel had a full time job which provided both medical benefits and a second source of income. After another year or so while Don and Rachel evaluated the alternatives, they decided to form a partnership by merging their practice with another accountant in the same town. This required a new office so now they were in a new 2000 square foot office with new leasehold improvements, new computers, a new telephone system and eleven people in the firm. What ever happened to the concept of a home-based business?

The partnership lasted a little over two years, but the key lesson Don learned and any small businessman or entrepreneur must learn is the ability to delegate work. Don just could not do everything by himself. The breakup of the partnership was untimely, but the monthly accounting clients and number of tax returns continued to grow and Don added professional staff with accounting degrees to cover the load. With a current office staff of seven plus himself, Don and Rachel are very pleased with the growth and success of their accounting firm since he started as a home-based business sixteen years ago. From that first bedroom office they have grown to about 750 individual tax returns a year, approximately 175 corporate tax returns and prepare monthly financial statements for close to 100 clients. Don's firm is probably the largest accounting service in our town.

EVALUATION

At fifty-seven, Don's next goal is to retire at sixty-two so he's got five years left to continue growing the firm and planning his transition into retirement. Somehow, I do not think he is going to handle retirement very well. I have never seen Don sit still for more than three minutes at a time. If he is not at the office, he is attending an accounting meeting or dropping in at the Chamber of Commerce to see what else needs to be done.

After working at home for eight years and now eight years in a normal office Don and Rachel have learned a tremendous amount. From a financial perspective, it probably took five years of growth after they moved into an office to net the same income he was earning at home due to the additional investment for the leasehold improvements, additional office furniture, and overhead.

"It was worth it! At home, Don just could not get away from the business." Rachel went on to say that he just couldn't mentally disassociate himself from work because work was always in the corner room. In addition, with so many clients in their home, home did not feel like home for Rachel either. They just had to make the transition to an office to separate their home life from their office life.

This is not always a problem for a home-based business if clients are not meeting in your home. An accounting service, however, does present this problem as it is a personal service. As a side comment, however, most of the home-based businesses interviewed for this book do not have clients in their home and do not want clients in their home.

The only way Don could have continued operating out of his home-based office would have been to determine a level of income and lifestyle he was comfortable with and limit his client growth. With a limited client list, Don could have continued to make some office calls to pick up the accounting work and limited the clients calling on him at home. The mental transition, however, between working at home and relaxing at home is a lot more difficult.

THE OFFICE

PHOTOGRAPHICS by Nico Pavan

PROFESSIONAL PHOTOGRAPHER

Nico Pavan, just celebrating his 30th birthday, grew up in Toronto, Canada with a father who produced commercials and videos, so it is no surprise that Nico eventually wound up being a freelance photographer. One summer, when Nico was thirteen his parents decided that it was unproductive for him to sit around the house, so they told Nico it was time to find a job. Nico's father had a friend that was a photographer and he could always use some help around his shop. He cleaned up, helped setup lights, and did general jobs. Nico never got paid, but he learned while he worked, and after working in the shop for a year and a half he had learned enough about photography to start taking his own pictures.

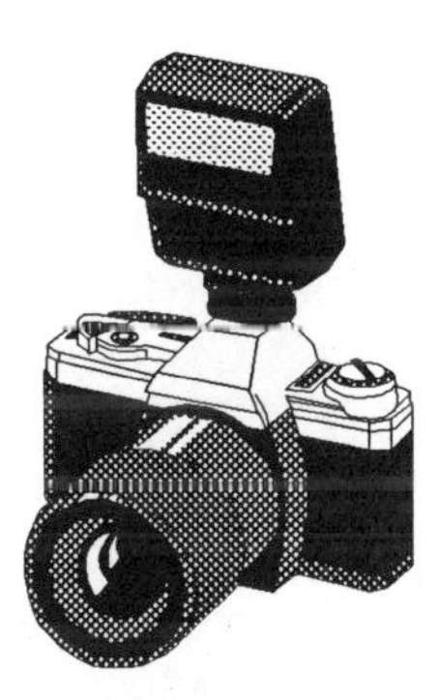

At fifteen, while still in school, he figured it was time he became his own boss. Nico, with another friend started their own freelance photography business. It wasn't big, but it was a start. Their marketing strategy was simple, they just called people on the telephone and would tell whoever answered that they had just won a FREE 8" x 10" photograph. They would ask, "*When would you like us to come over and take your photograph for you?*" People thought not only do I get a free photograph but they come to my home to take it. What a deal! Of course being fifteen, neither of the "partners" had a car. No problem, they just grabbed their cameras, lighting equipment and hopped on the bus. The bus went everywhere. The people were thrilled with their free photograph, the excellent quality and "*didn't little sister's pose come out good?*" They liked them so well that the average sale of other poses taken was $350! Nico and his partner thought they had struck gold, and it didn't even seem like working. They were getting paid for enjoying their hobby.

Nico continued to freelance his photographic skills during college. He did so well with his business that he paid his college expenses with the money he earned. He went to a four year photography college in Toronto where he learned all he needed to know about photography to become a master at his craft.

After graduation, Nico moved to Tampa with his family and started his own full time freelance photography business. As Nico says, "*I shoot just about anything, but I don't do weddings.*" His photographs have appeared in several local newspapers and he does work all over the country for magazines, product promotion, model portfolios, or in-house corporate newsletters, just to name a few. With a love of photography, Nico also teaches photography and darkroom techniques at Baywinds Learning Centres, Inc. in Tampa. Baywinds offers adult education classes throughout the Tampa Bay area on specialty hobbies, professional interest areas, and recreational topics.

Talking about his different photography assignments, it became very clear that a lot more goes into a photograph then just pointing and shooting the camera.

Shooting a photograph for a helicopter brochure, for example, the company wanted the helicopter up in the air so there would be only the blue sky background. He had to take the pictures from another helicopter. It was cloudy that day so they had to go above the clouds, to 10,000 feet. How do you take a picture from a helicopter so the picture doesn't look like it was shot through the window? Of course, you have to lean out of the helicopter...at 10,000 feet! He did get some great pictures though.

He also had a unique assignment shooting the Joey Chitwood race car. The Chitwoods are famous for their daredevil car driving performances, especially driving with the car tipped up on the two side tires. Where was the product promotion on the car? Of course, on the underside. How does one take a picture of the underside of the car? Well if it is on a Chitwood car it's easy, just have them tip the car up on the side two wheels and drive down the track. How do you take a picture of a car tipped on it's side driving down a track? It's easy Nico said, "*I just laid on top of a van and had someone drive alongside the car.*" He then went on to add, " *I had to get the shots they wanted on the first try. The Chitwood's only wanted to go around the track once, because driving on the edge of the tires wore them out so they had to be changed after every lap.*" Maybe that's why we have to keep replacing the tires on our two sons' cars.

Nico is also somewhat of a photographic inventor, and uses his new ideas for extra income. If he can't find equipment that is readily available or is too expensive he makes it himself. Other photographers have purchased some of his inventions for their own use.

One of his inventions was a sound sensor device that would release the shutter and take pictures remotely. The sound sensor can even be set at different decibel levels. He designed the sensor specifically for the Space Shuttle launches. No one can get closer than three miles to the shuttle when it is launched, so all the cameras have to be set up to shoot remotely. Since Nico's device can be set at different decibel levels he used it to set up several different cameras focused at different heights so the cameras would shoot the shuttle as it rose. The cameras shot the pictures at different heights because the sound decibels change with the height of the launch. I was impressed.

Nico still talks about his photographic work with the enthusiasm of the fifteen year old boy who started a photographic business using the local bus. Freelancing gives him the creative freedom to take only the jobs that he really wants to do, and by working out of his house he has kept his independence and cut the costs of having to pay rent for a studio. He no longer has a dining room, but every job has limitations. The day we were at his house he was doing a product promotion and had the display and all his lighting equipment set up in the dining room. He uses his livingroom for a waiting room and conference room. His office is in a spare bedroom. On his office walls are some of his photographs, one being of the Space Shuttle taken by his sound sensor device.

Utilizing an answering machine that he can call from other locations, Nico gets and returns messages even when he is on location. In his case he does not feel that an answering service or beeper is necessary as most of the jobs he works on have a reasonable lead time and a call back the next day is alright. He has a personal computer and dot matrix printer that he uses to do all his invoicing, record keeping and correspondence.

For direct mail marketing Nico uses sample photographs that he has taken, with his advertising on the picture. Using photographs is cost effective, provides information about his business, and also provides a sample of his work. He has received a lot of response from his direct mail marketing and always has a new promotion in the works. His next promotion will be sample pictures on coffee mugs. Hopefully, the person will have the cup on their desk all the time, which has Nico's name and telephone number in plain view. Through trade shows and conferences, Nico also works at keeping and enlarging his pool of referrals, as photographers often refer each other for particular specialty shots or geographic locations.

PRESSLER & ASSOCIATES, INC.

MANUFACTURER'S AGENT

Don Pressler markets petroleum distribution equipment and supplies to petroleum wholesale distributors throughout the State of Florida. With exclusive marketing rights for the state from six different manufacturers', Don has covered the state for the last two and a half years out of his home-based office.

Marketing on a commission basis, Pressler & Associates, Inc., receives a fee for all equipment and supplies shipped into the state by the manufacturers he represents. Specifically identifying his target market as wholesale distributors, Don narrowed his customer base to about two hundred companies who in turn sell to approximately 10,000 existing gas stations, large commercial customers, and quick service oil and lubrication stations.

With a degree in Business Administration from Oglethorp College in Atlanta, Ga., and a lifetime of sales and marketing experience it was only natural that Don established a marketing firm when he was finally ready to start his own company. He initially got his marketing training with Lanier Business Products selling copiers, dictation, and word processing equipment for two and a half years. From Lanier, Don spent the next couple years with Michelin Tire Company working with Michelin Distributors throughout the southern United States. It was then three years as District Manager for the State of Florida with Kawasaki Motorcycles and two more years representing the Sunfish Division of AMF Marine throughout the state.

In 1981, he moved to Tampa to start an industrial sales division for a petroleum equipment distributor. Marketing throughout Florida, Don soon knew all the petroleum equipment and supplies dealers in the state. Approached by another distributor in 1986, Don worked for another couple of years before finally deciding to start his own company as a manufacturer's representative in January of 1989. Having knowledge of the existing customer base and contact with the manufacturers, it was a natural transition and mutually beneficial as he began marketing petroleum equipment and supplies for manufacturers who were too small to have a direct sales force but needed to increase their marketing presence.

Don could not have picked a worse time as new construction of gas stations fell significantly because of the recession in the early 1990's. Maintenance and upgrading of existing stations to comply with Federal Environmental Regulations, however, provided a base of sales to grow on.

MARKETING

Having a well defined target market of wholesale petroleum distributors, Don primarily markets through direct sales calls and direct mailing. Averaging about two weeks a month "out of town," Don divides the State into zones and calls on existing accounts to ensure a continual market presence. While the travel gets old quickly, Don tries to limit his overnight stays to about six or seven a month. By leaving on Monday morning and returning Thursday night he tries to maintain a balance between work and a home life.

The remaining two weeks each month, Don makes calls within commuting distance of his home and gets caught up on paper work and direct mailings. From an administrative standpoint, most of the petroleum equipment and supplies are ordered by the distributors direct from the manufacturers and shipped directly to the distributors. Billing is also done by the manufacturers so most of Don's office work is limited to following up technical product questions, delivery problems, or an occasional credit or collections problem.

In addition to calling on existing distributors to provide technical and market support, Don calls on engineers and architects who design new gas stations or commercial fuel distribution centers to introduce new products and equipment changes. He also calls on Environmental Protection Agencies to introduce equipment and go through  the process of getting EPA approval from all the appropriate agencies which often conflict in jurisdiction. Since EPA approval is required for equipment installed in each jurisdiction, Don calls on City, County, State, and Federal Agencies to cover all the bases.

Trade Shows are also a source of industry information and marketing, so Don attends the Florida Petroleum Marketers' Annual Convention and helps at the booths setup by the manufacturers he represents. He also attends several national trade shows a year to stay current on technology and products available in the industry.

Direct mail is a significant help in staying in contact with his accounts. Using an IBM compatible personal computer, 24 pin Panasonic printer, copier, and a word processing system (PFS First Choice), Don sends out new product announcements, mails special promotions, or technical product information to his accounts. A fax machine in his office and a car phone also ensure Don is readily available to any distributor needing to contact him. With a limited customer base of long term existing clients and a membership list from the Florida Petroleum Marketers Association, his direct mail is cost effective and manageable.

GROWTH

Having established his customer base, the next step in terms of growth is to add additional manufacturers to support. Provided the manufacturers are not marketing competing products to his existing lines, the additional products should be complimentary to his existing marketing effort. Growth, then, is a function of an improving economy, increased gas station construction, and additional product offerings. A second alternative, is to add additional personnel and expand his territory to include additional states. From a sales standpoint, Don can adequately cover the State of Florida, but he has been offered additional states by several of his existing manufacturers.

Expansion now becomes a significant question and requires a cash investment to establish a marketing representative in another state, an investment in office equipment and working capital as Don has to cover all his personal and corporate marketing expenses. Adding an additional sales person, therefore, would require covering the person's salary, travel expenses, a car allowance, and the office expenses until commissions generated by sales in the state cover the costs. Don would also face the additional challenge and expense of training and managing an out of state employee.

Expansion almost begins to defeat part of the intangible value of having a home-based business. Product expansion through adding additional product lines would require almost no additional investment and little marketing time. Territorial and employee expansion, on the other hand, would require a significant investment in working capital and managerial time.

RISING STAR PRODUCTIONS

LIVE MUSIC & KARAOKE

Chris Cook has been singing, dancing, and playing musical instruments since high school in a small Florida town. Playing four instruments and marching in the High School Band, Chris spent his spare time playing guitar and singing in a local rock band. He had his dream, it was just a question of how to become a professional singer?

BACKGROUND

After finishing high school, Chris started college while working part time to earn school expenses. Two years later, it was time for the U.S. Air Force and a chance to see the world. After basic training, Chris was stationed in Sacramento, California as a telecommunications technician. The Air Force, however, only served as a training ground to enhance Chris's musical skills and further his ambition to become a professional singer.

He auditioned and won a spot singing in the Tops & Blues, a prestigious Air Force singing group. The groups' purpose was to entertain at various military bases around the world as a morale booster to the servicemen and women. Similar to a USO tour, the Tops & Blues, performed Las Vegas style reviews and sang contemporary music. What a way to see the world.

While not on tour or working in communications, Chris got his FCC (Federal Communications Commission) License and worked part time at a local Sacramento television station as an equipment technician. Still not satisfied, Chris also began performing in local musical theater productions and singing and playing music on weekends at some of the local nightclubs.

At the end of his military service, Chris decided to stay in the San Francisco/Sacramento area and pursue his singing and hopefully a theater career. With a couple of years of singing and performing on a part time basis, Chris was ready to become a full time singer. He landed a permanent position singing at a local nightclub as "happy hour" entertainment, prior to touring bands hired as the main attraction for the evening crowd. After two years of singing and playing his guitar, Chris had added enough electronic equipment to his act to advertise himself as a "one man band."

He soon replaced the touring bands and became the lead entertainment during the evening. For the next three years he continued with the club until the ownership changed. During this time he was also playing a few other clubs and composing background music for commercials. After singing for five years at the club, he started touring nightclubs, bars, and casinos in the Northern California and Nevada area singing and playing.

Marketing was based on professional referrals, a video demonstration tape which he had produced, personal sales calls, and professional agents. Although agents usually took 10%-20% of the engagement fees, they supplemented his own marketing efforts. After ten years of singing and playing nightclubs in California and northern Nevada, he was ready for a change and a little slower pace.

Chris and his wife decided to return to the west coast of Florida where Chris had grown up. After ten years of professionally singing. Chris had gotten used to the freedom and flexibility of being his own boss. With a room full of electronic equipment an his trusty guitar, Chris was back on the road promoting his singing at local beach clubs, dinner clubs, and bars. Playing two or three nights a week in different towns, Chris started to notice signs advertising "KARAOKE TUESDAY NIGHT" or KARAOKE FRIDAY NIGHT." *I couldn't believe how often I was seeing signs for Karaoke. They must really be a popular band,*" said Chris.

KARAOKE

Karaoke opened a whole new world. In the past, audience participation had been limited to dancing while a band or singer entertained them. A few individuals might ask to sing, but it was rare because the person had to know the words to the song as well as being able to sing. With Karaoke, the entire audience can sing and participate.

In Karaoke, a compact laser disc player plays prerecorded music while a television connected to the CD player shows a video with the words to the song across the bottom. The participants do not even have to know the tune, the words to the song are highlighted on the video in tune with the song. Singing Karaoke is as easy as following the little red light.

Chris immediately saw the potential. What a combination, professional singing and participation by the crowd through Karaoke. Chris purchased the necessary equipment to add Karoake to his evening show. The investment in equipment was expensive, but he already had all the necessary sound equipment and there was still a little room on his Visa card.

Marketing suddenly became a lot easier. Instead of a lounge or club relying totally on the professional skill of his singing, Karaoke provided alternative entertainment. Combined with his ability to professionally sing and provide backup music with his equipment, Karaoke provided a competitive edge in marketing his services. *"Karaoke is here to stay. I even have individuals who rent my home studio to practice singing,"* says Chris.

Audience involvement seems to make the evening a lot more fun for everyone. With a drink or two, everyone thinks they are Frank Sinatra. I originally met Chris at a Karaoke night, and it's a lot of fun. The evening was like a three hour "Gong Show." Some of the singers from the audience were really good. Others were terrible, but had a great time singing anyway. There is nothing better then a group of five and not a single one can carry a tune.

Chris has made a sizeable investment that Karaoke is here to stay and the audiences will continue participating. I have to admit, though, as fun as Karaoke is, it is still nice to hear Chris sing professionally. A couple of "Bud lights" can make you feel like a singer, but only Karaoke can get you on stage.

ROYAL PALM PLANNING

FINANCIAL PLANNING & INVESTMENT COUNSEL

"...manage your income more efficiently, feel better about your investments, and enjoy the satisfaction and peace of mind that comes from knowing you have a sound, comprehensive financial plan.", reads Steve Madson's company brochure.

As a fee only financial planner, Steve Madson, at forty eight, is in a position most of us would envy.

With the New York Stock Exchange quotes flashing by on cable television, Value Line corporate evaluations behind the desk, an IBM compatible 386 based personal computer online to Telescan (a stock database) and hooked up to a Laserjet printer, Steve works out of his home office providing personal financial planning. For a set annual fee of eight tenths of one percent (.8%) of your investment assets, he provides comprehensive financial planning that includes stock investment counseling, insurance, budgeting, retirement, and estate planning.

Steve got interested in investments at the University of Wisconsin where he had a double major in Business and English. Following a tour in army military intelligence, Steve went to work with the State of Minnesota Human Resources Department. With four years of experience in recruiting and interviewing, Steve then joined the Minnesota Mining and Manufacturing Company in their personnel department. Initially in recruiting and outplacement counseling, he later transferred to the marketing side doing sales and strategic planning proposals.

While there, he saw the human side of corporate strategies while providing outplacement counseling to employees being discharged or laid off for a multitude of reasons ranging from incompetence to corporate reorganizations. Single, approaching thirty, and with nine years of active investing in the stock market,

Steve decided it was time to live his own dream. With a lifelong ambition to write a novel based on his love of English and Literature gained while in college, minimal expenses, and stock investments enough to last for three years he decided to devote the next three years to managing his stock portfolio and to writing his novel.

Three years and a much smaller savings account later, Steve began teaching business courses for the St. Paul Technical College while continuing to write and rebuild his investment portfolio. In addition, Steve also completed the American Express/IDS Financial Planning Training Program getting licensed as a Registered Financial Advisor. Rather than go to work with IDS (Investors Diversified Services) as a financial planner, he decided to continue working on his own. With a talent for investment analysis and stock investing, Steve began charging his clients for his financial planning advice. Working out of his home, he continued teaching, writing, and building his financial planning business.

Almost forty, a new wife and about to be a father for the first time, and the weather getting colder every winter in Minneapolis, Steve and his spouse decided it was time to move south. Steve's wife, an executive with an insurance company, applied for and accepted a transfer to Florida to help in opening a new sales office.

After ten years of teaching, writing, and running his home-based financial planning firm, Steve was not physically tied to a specific geographical location. With Florida sunshine, sand, and palm trees replacing the snow, **Royal Palm Planning** was born along with continuing to teach business courses for Tampa College and an occasional rewrite or two of the now 900 page novel. A six inch thick manuscript and a dozen or so rejection letters still hadn't discouraged the dream to finish his novel.

EVALUATION

Like all personal service companies, the hardest part about a home-based financial planning service is the marketing. The business relationship is usually started and nurtured based on a personal relationship between the parties. As a result, the most common source of new accounts are client referrals and personal contacts. Due to the personal contact required, traditional advertising such as flyers or published advertisements have limited value. Speaking engagements at different professional associations or civic groups, however, do provide an opportunity to establish a sense of credibility and an occasional client.

A well written brochure is available and plants the idea of personal financial planning in a potential client or referral. The actual client development, however, still comes down to a one on one personal relationship. This relationship is necessary because part of the financial planning service is a limited power-of-attorney for Steve to initiate buy and sell orders for stock through the clients brokerage account. Tied in with a cash management account at a stockbroker's office, Steve can buy and sell for the client to maximize timing opportunities in the marketplace when the client is unavailable. With the tie between the stock and cash management account (CMA), Steve is able to eliminate any fraud concerns as all sell proceeds flow directly into the brokerage controlled CMA account. Purchase orders are also paid out of the CMA so no cash flows through Royal Palm Planning.

As a fee only planner, Steve does provide the security to a client that his recommendations or trades are based on the client's best interest. Unlike a normal brokerage house, insurance agent, or many well known financial planning companies where commissions are generated, the client never knows to what extent recommendations are made based on the commission generated and not the merits of the specific investment. In the industry this is known as "churning" or turning over the stock in a portfolio just to generate commissions. After seventeen years of writing, teaching, and providing financial planning services, I did not even ask Steve if he ever thought about getting a regular job? I didn't want to embarrass myself.

SALINGS OBEDIENCE & TRAINING

FAMILY DOG TRAINING

With a lifetime of loving and training dogs, Brenda Saling is on the go every day caring for her husband, four children, eight dogs, and her home-based dog training business. Working out of a garage converted into an office, Brenda is clearly doing what she enjoys. With close to a hundred awards, her walls are covered with ribbons, medals, and trophies won in AKC (American Kennel Club) competition. As I sat interviewing her, two German Shepherds were on one side, two Shelties were in and out of their crates by the fireplace, a miniature Pinscher was in her lap, and a Doberman Pinscher came in to see what was going on. I will admit, however, that they were all extremely well behaved considering I was a little overwhelmed. I was impressed, though, when Brenda asked if I would like a soda. The Shepherd opened the refrigerator door, one Sheltie held the glass and the other poured.

Going on her seventh year in business, Brenda got started as a result of her love for dogs. In her early twenties, Brenda had a dog and obedience trainer work with herself and her pet Doberman just to establish a better relationship with her pet. The trainer would come to Brenda's home and work just with her and her pet. During the training she got to be friends with the consultant and the relationship continued afterward with the trainer encouraging Brenda to get involved in learning about dog training. The friendship did get Brenda interested in dog training and led to an interest in AKC competition. Brenda began studying all the AKC rules and training competition requirements. She was soon training her own dog and entering training competition at AKC Trials. The AKC competition really honed her enthusiasm and interest in training methods and techniques.

As her dog placed in more trials and gained increasingly higher levels of certification, Brenda began going around the neighborhood training relatives', friends', and neighbor's dogs to practice her training techniques. Her friends soon began telling Brenda she should start charging money for her training lessons. Up to now, it had all been a fun and a challenging hobby.

With a very supportive husband, and teenage children who were already reasonably well trained, she decided to give it a try. Brenda began working individually with clients who were usually referred by existing friends. Brenda's primary emphasis continues to be private training sessions in the owner's home, but she has also expanded to teaching a series of Training & Obedience Workshops through a local pet store. With attendance limited to six participants and their pets, the workshops meet for an hour one evening a week, for an eight week period. She often schedules three workshops a week. She teaches two and her husband teaches the third.

In addition to her basic Dog Obedience Workshops, Brenda also offers a special "Puppy Course" for puppies and their new owners. For experienced owners, Brenda offers an Advanced Competition Workshop for those owners interested in competing in AKC Trials. Brenda offers a wealth of AKC competition experience as well as training techniques and tips on the specific routines required in AKC competition, based on eleven years of competing on a state wide basis.

While AKC competition is fun, Brenda says, "*My heart's desire is to teach people to have an understanding of dog behavior so they will have a dog they can live with.*" Brenda has also gone out of her way to get involved in the local Humane Society and provides dog obedience displays at local Humane Society charity events. You will even find Brenda showing her dogs at local retirement homes as a form of pet therapy. "*They just love the dogs, and it's my way of giving back to the community,*" says Brenda.

MARKETING

As her business has grown, Brenda has expanded her marketing to include business cards which she hands out. Cards are also available at a number of veterinarian offices in the area. By utilizing the veterinarians or centers of influence with potential customers, Brenda is getting her service to potential clients who already have an interest in her service.

In drafting this interview, I called a veterinarian who is a friend and asked about providing business cards or brochures of complimentary products or services. As a general rule, he said they do not make available business cards or brochures for other businesses unless they recommend and are familiar with the product. "*We get two or three people a month who would like to leave cards for our customers and we normally don't accept them. We don't want to risk losing a customer who has a bad experience with a product which they assume was endorsed by us because they got the card or brochure at our office."* He went on to add, that in a few cases if they have confidence in the service and feel it would be a benefit to their customers then they have the cards available. They do have business cards available from Salings Obedience & Dog Training, but before accepting them they checked on the reputation of Brenda with some of their current customers and visited Brenda while in a Training Workshop.

EVALUATION

From a marketing standpoint, Brenda has primarily relied on workshop announcements at local pet shops, business cards, referrals, and a yellow page advertisement. All have been successful in providing leads, with referrals, of course, being the best source.

With a limited number of potential dog owners who purchase dogs in our local community each year, Brenda recognizes the need to expand to Tampa and the other surrounding communities. In expanding her service area, Brenda is currently working on a trifold 8 1/2 by 11 inch brochure which she can mail to calls generated from her yellow page advertising and cards. In addition, Brenda will have the Brochures to leave for potential customers as she visits pet shops and veterinarians outside the local community. The brochure, stressing eleven years of AKC competition and seven years in the dog training business should add more credibility than a simple business card can convey.

In the local community, she has been able to primarily rely on her reputation and personal enthusiasm. As she expands, her flyers, brochures and printed literature about her company have to leave the potential client with the same feeling of professional competence, experience, and enthusiasm as would a personal visit with Brenda.

Brenda's dogs have even appeared on local television commercials. This type of mass advertising can only enhance her local reputation. She should also consider a local newspaper article on Dog Obedience Training and a small six or eight page pamphlet on Dog Training to hand to potential customers. The more printed literature Brenda can put in the hands of potential customers, the more it enhances her reputation as a professional dog trainer.

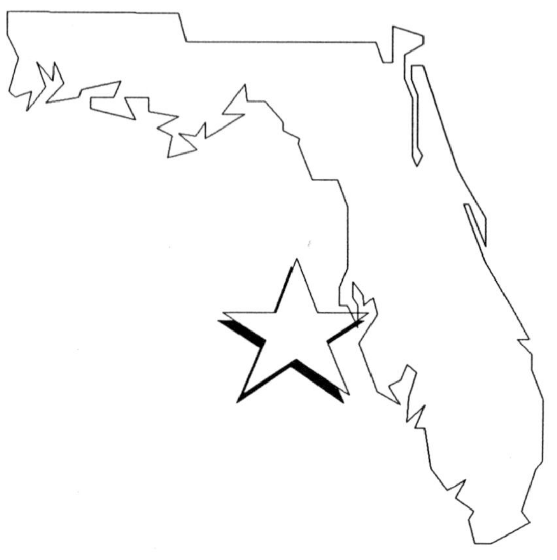

SUN SPECIALISTS, INC.

HAWAIIAN TROPIC DISTRIBUTOR

With a bachelors degree in Economics and a Law Degree, there can not possibly be a more unusual background for the number one distributor of sun tan lotion on the west coast of Florida.

Skip Moore started college as a Chemical Engineering major and then switched to Economics before finishing with a degree from Auburn University. From there, it was three more years at the University of Florida Law School. Finishing in 1968 and passing the Florida Bar Exam in 1969, Skip began work with a local law firm, ready for everything life had to offer.

Just a few months later, Skip went to bed one evening with a severe headache and the next morning his vision was blurry to the point he could not read. Everything Skip had worked for suddenly changed. Unable to read legal documents or focus on pending cases, his law career came to a sudden end. For the next year he tried a number of local jobs while visiting doctors and trying to figure out what to do next.

From a medical perspective the most plausible explanation he received was that a small blood vein associated with his optic nerves had burst due to the headache and the disruption in the blood supply had impacted his vision. It sounded like a reasonable explanation, but the doctors could not do anything about it.

A chance conversation gave Skip an avenue of hope. While talking with a neighbor's teenage son in Daytona Beach, Skip asked what his plans for the summer were? About to start college as a freshman in the fall, he replied that he was going to the beach to sell suntan lotion all day. A dream job for any student. Skip asked how he was going to make any money selling suntan lotion? *"I expect to make about $6,000 this summer, which is all I need for school expenses next year,"* he replied.

Skip stood there in disbelief, but he went along to the beach to see if it was possible. Skip said, *"I watched my neighbor's son all day and couldn't believe how many dollars and bottles of suntan lotion changed hands."* Skip and the young man then went to an old gas station and a high school chemistry teacher, Ron Rice, was mixing lotion in fifty gallon drums and hand filling suntan lotion bottles which college kids would sell along the beach the next day. *"I couldn't believe the operation or the amount of money being made."*

Skip filled up his trunk with suntan lotion out of that garage, gave Ron a check, and said he would be back when he sold that load. That is the short version of how Skip bacame the distributor for the west coast of Florida and began selling Hawaiian Tropic Suntan Lotion. The hardest part, however, was what to do next?

MARKETING

Living in an apartment in Tampa, Florida with his wife, Skip decided to market Hawaiian Tropic through beach retailers rather than trying to sell one bottle at a time. With most of his inventory in his bedroom closet, Skip kept enough in his car trunk to make a few sales. Heading for Clearwater Beach, he began calling on every beachfront retail store.

"What is that stuff called?" *"No, we're not interested!"* *"Come back next week."* *"Get out of here."* It was a long day, but Skip was back the next day, and the day after. It was extremely slow at first because the number one selling suntan lotion at the time was Coppertone and no one had ever heard of Hawaiian Tropic. Unlike a lot of one time sales, the retail business for suntan lotion is based on a long term relationship in which ongoing inventory has to be provided to the retail outlet. No one wanted to take a chance on a kid selling Hawaiian something, who might not be here tomorrow.

Skip had to do something to get the stores interested. He and his wife, Judy, an elementary school teacher in special education, decided to try creating customer demand for Hawaiian Tropic by passing out free samples on the beach. Armed with a smile and squirt dispenser of suntan lotion, Judy would go up and down the beach offering free suntan lotion. With an innate talent to make people feel comfortable, Judy, who later in her career was honored as the Hillsborough County Teacher of the Year and Outstanding Educator in Florida, began introducing Hawaiian Tropic.

With a commitment to making this work, Skip would also take a squirt bottle and hit the beach offering suntan lotion, but found he was not as successful. Somehow, the young girls did not want Skip rubbing Hawaiian Tropic on their shoulders!!! Having learned the secret to passing out lotion samples, as Skip continued to expand, he hired young beautiful girls to pass out samples at the beach and the beach stores soon began having customers asking for Hawaiian Tropic.

Skip, meanwhile, continued calling on the beach stores and slowly began getting stores to carry Hawaiian Tropic. Although a slow start, as Skip could have hired college kids to sell individual bottles on the beach, he was determined to build an ongoing business not just make a few dollars for the summer.

The second secret to success which Skip capitalized on was the supply side of the suntan lotion business. Up to this point, suntan lotion was primarily sold to the beach stores in bulk orders by salesmen who represented the major companies. A retailer would order lotion by the case to be delivered through normal shipping and distribution channels which might take months from the order date to the date of delivery. Skip kept an inventory in his trunk and delivery took ten minutes. He even stocked, arranged the display, and serviced the account on a regular basis (usually weekly). Skip ensured the store always had suntan lotion and simply left the store an invoice after refilling their display.

In essence, he made it easy for the retail store to do business with him. Having inventory in his trunk even led to one of his largest accounts. Expanding along the west coast of Florida, Skip called on a new drug store about to open in Sarasota who had an initial inventory of Coppertone suntan lotion on order. With the grand opening scheduled for the next day, they still had not received the suntan lotion. Skip happened to make a sales call that day and guess what he had in his trunk? He brought lotion in, set up a Hawaiian Tropic display, and for years that account has been one of the largestest sellers of Hawaiian Tropic on the west coast of Florida.

At another account, he called on the owner every Friday for two years before he got his first order. He was in the area servicing his other accounts on that day and made it a point to stop in and say hello. *"I wanted that owner to know I was there like clockwork, in case he ever had trouble with his normal supplier."* After two years, the owner finally had Skip set up a Hawaiian Tropic display and today the families vacation together.

Making trips back and forth to Daytona Beach to resupply his bedroom closet, Skip finally bought a small home and the inventory expanded to the garage and he used one of the bedrooms as an office. The weekly trips to Daytona also expanded as Skip graduated from a car trunk of inventory to a small enclosed utility trailer which he pulled and had **HAWAIIAN TROPIC** painted on the sides.

Skip's first major break came in 1973, two years after he started selling Hawaiian Tropic. He had been calling on Maas Brothers, a large upscale department store chain based in Florida and they finally agreed to try Hawaiian Tropic in just three of their stores. The initial inventory sold out in just two days. *"I was even surprised as I had thought about buying the inventory myself just to get sales started,"* said Skip. By the third order, Maas Brothers had Hawaiian Tropic in all their stores and later began to include the lotion in their Home Cosmetics Catalog which they mailed to all their customers. Maas Brothers added to the credibility of Hawaiian Tropic and provided advertising which Skip could not afford, as well as the direct increase in sales volume. It was still pretty early in the history of Hawaiian Tropic and well before the corporate office was doing any national advertising.

During the two years Skip had been working fifteen hour days to make his business a success, his sight had slowly returned as alternative veins and capillaries had expanded to compensate for the injury. His vision was back to normal after about eighteen months, but by then, Skip was committed to his own business. Working with his wife had been a tremendous growing and sharing experience and he did not want to go back to a corporate or law office.

The next step in his marketing plan was attendance and participation as an exhibitor at trade shows attended by the retail store owners. Skip always had "giveaways" for the attendees with the name Hawaiian Tropic on them just to keep the name in front of them. Trade Shows also gave Skip an opportunity to meet new store owners.

Skip continued operating out of his garage for five years before he outgrew his home and finally bought a small commercial building which he renovated into an office and warehouse. That building was finally replaced and today Skip operates out of a 4500 square foot building with eleven employees. Salesmen still carry inventory in their cars, unload the lotion and stock the displays. According to Skip, *"Customer Service is the most important thing in this business. The store has to know they can depend on you."*

EVALUATION

It has been twenty years since Skip met Ron Rice, and Hawaiian Tropic has since grown to become a tremendous success story. The success, however, was built on getting one retail store at a time. Skip succeeded because he was committed. With his back to the wall, Skip found the courage to call on just one more retail store. He found that courage every hour and every day. Skip likes to give credit and thanks the people he has had the good fortune to meet in the industry and the employees that have worked with him. *I was just lucky to be in the right place at the right time,*" he said.

I'm not sure Skip gives himself enough credit. That one lucky store who happened to run out of a competitor's product on the day Skip happened to be there, or the day the customer finally agreed out of the blue to try Hawaiian Tropic are not luck. It was the one hundred and four sales calls Skip made every Friday for two years that created the opportunity. It was the fifty calls that did not succeed to create the one that just "happened" to need the product on that day. We make our own luck with **HARD WORK** and **PERSISTENCE.**

In Skip's case, Hawaiian Tropic did not make him a success, Skip and many other distributors just like him made Hawaiian Tropic a success.

In addition to Hawaiian Tropic, for the last fourteen years Skip has also been a distributor for Crown Sun Glasses. Utilizing the same marketing force and warehouse distribution, Skip has helped build Crown Sun Glasses into a nationally known brand. The addition of Crown, also helped Skip maximize the effectiveness of his sales people and spread his overhead over a larger base of product sales.

WALSH & ASSOCIATES

WHOLESALE DISTRIBUTION CONSULTANTS

Paul Walsh was five years old when he knew what he wanted to be. No fireman or policeman, a W.T. Grant Company store manager just like his dad, a thirty year career manager with the company.

After graduation from high school, Paul joined the U.S. Navy and upon his discharge in 1965 joined The W.T. Grant Company Management Training Program. Three years later he was managing his first retail store in Jacksonville, Florida. From then on it was charge, charge, charge with six successive promotions each time to a larger store.

Ten and a half years later in 1975 it all came to an end as The W.T. Grant Company filed for Chapter 11 Bankruptcy protection. Thirty one years old, married, two children, a mortgage, a fistful of The W.T. Grant Company stock certificates, and ten years invested in a company career.

Shocked, Paul knew right then that security is what you build for yourself. As a reminder, he still has The W.T. Grant Company Stock Certificates.

Landing on his feet, Paul joined the Eli Witt Company in Tampa, Florida and began a fourteen year career which progressed from General Manager of an area distribution facility to Director of Marketing, Director of Purchasing, Vice President of Marketing and finally Regional Vice President of Operations. The thought of independence and owning his own business, however, continued to grow as he progressed through management.

An avid outdoor sportsman, Paul made the decision to buy a company while on a "deer stand" during a hunting trip. Forty three years old, he gave himself two years to conduct a market search of potential companies to purchase, line up an investor group to provide the equity investment, and make sure his personal financial plans and affairs were in order. As the two years progressed, he also worked with the officers of the Eli Witt Company, sharing his plans to purchase a company so Eli Witt could plan an orderly transition as Paul planned to resign at the end of 1989.

PERSONAL FINANCIAL PLANS

In 1979, Paul had built a custom designed home in a suburb of Tampa, Florida and as time passed, the home continued to satisfy his needs. As he began to anticipate the purchase of a business, the low payments on his home which he had now been in for ten years provided a base on which to build his personal financial plans. The first step in his financial plan was to payoff all consumer debt with the exception of the house mortgage (a 9.5%, fixed rate, thirty year mortgage is hard to beat). The next step was to increase his personal savings and investment rate to provide a financial cushion as he projected a growth period in the early years of business ownership during which his salary (if any) would be limited.

As events unfolded, Paul was right on track with his planned resignation date. By the end of 1989, Paul had no consumer debt, a $500 a month house payment, and liquid investments in stock and money market accounts totaling $85,000. As an added benefit, which he had not originally planned on, the Eli Witt Company negotiated a severance package based on his fourteen years in management with the company in which they planned to extend his salary, benefits, and provide office space and secretarial services for an additional seven months past his resignation date.

In evaluating his outgoing expenses, he felt he could get by on a minimum annual cash flow of $30,000 or $2,500 a month.   Paul could not have planned his personal finances any better.

BUSINESS FINANCIAL PLANS

Paul immediately began to develop the criteria to purchase an existing company preferably in the distribution/retail business. Based on the equity commitment of investors Paul had known in his business career, he narrowed his search to closely held companies which had a market value in the range of $2,000,000 to $6,000,000.

Of the purchase price, part would be funded through the equity commitments and the balance would be funded through bank debt based on the company assets, a thorough business plan, and the existing track record of the company to pay the debt payments.

All initially went well as Paul began an assessment of companies meeting his financing and growth requirements. The end result, however, was elusive as Paul was unable to finalize a purchase during the two year time frame he had committed to himself and the Eli Witt Company. Several purchases came close, but the price negotiations fell through or bank financing couldn't be obtained (this was not a great time to look for bank financing for small businesses due to the commercial bank concerns with the Savings and Loan bailout, increased FDIC audit pressures on loan documentation, and the growing recession). Paul was committed to his resignation date and being on his own, however, as he knew a company would come along which met his criteria.

CONSULTING

Paul had never considered consulting as a business, but during the networking phase of looking for companies which might be available to purchase, a business acquaintance offered a consulting engagement. After resigning from Eli Witt, Paul decided to give it a try. After all, how could he turn it down? A consulting rate of $500.00 a day ($62.50 an hour) plus all expenses for travel, meals, lodging, and out of pocket expenses incurred on behalf of his client. In essence, Paul's only investment to get started was the cost of printing a set of business cards.

This consulting had potential! Working on the consulting engagement in two-day increments with a third day for travel to minimize his travel time, Paul had plenty of time in his home office and began calling other business contacts to obtain consulting engagements or referrals.

By the end of the first year, Paul was amazed! He had billed $42,000 in consulting fees and his only expenses were long distance charges and business cards.

In addition to the initial consulting engagement with each company to identify specific business problems and write an Implementation Plan to address the problems, Paul is also involved in the implementation of his recommendations by monitoring and evaluating the results. Being involved in the implementation provides immediate feedback on the consulting recommendations to the company and Paul, and also provides a source of ongoing business as Paul is not marketing a few days or a week of consulting time, but is developing an ongoing relationship. With this experience in mind, Paul entered his second year of consulting with a more defined business plan for his personal consulting business.

His marketing plan began to get more professional with the preparation of a brochure outlining his consulting services, a few mailings to referrals and potential clients, advertisements in industry trade journals, and a commitment to building a home-based consulting business. In assessing his marketing, the response from trade journal advertisements was nominal. His clients so far, have all come from referrals or personal contacts. The aim of the mailings, however, is a long term commitment to make himself better known as a consultant in the industry. Although trade association meetings are held, he has not attended any and has not gotten involved in speaking or writing for the available trade journals or conferences.

Pricing got a little more aggressive with an increase in billing rates to $650.00 a day ($81.25 per hour) plus expenses. Paul has also established a goal of $800.00 per day which he feels is in line with better known consultants in his specific area of expertise and industry.

EVALUATION

In evaluating his second year of consulting, his billing for the year should be in the range of $70,000-$80,000 based on his current engagements. He has established a goal of $100,000 a year.

From an operations standpoint, Paul has no plans to get involved in preparing the Consulting Implementation Plans or in sending out the mailing. He has established a relationship with a local secretarial service (also home-based) who does all his word processing. With this approach, his only ongoing expense will be marketing and secretarial services to support his marketing effort as preparation of his Consulting Reports are rebilled to the clients. From an investment standpoint, an answering machine, a separate phone line and a fax machine are projected. But so far, they have not been critical.

In concluding our interview, I asked if he missed the corporate environment, the business lunches, the power and prestige associated with corporate management, and if he would consider going back?

Paul said he had just turned down an opportunity to be Vice President of Sales & Marketing for a company but suggested he was, however, available to do consulting. He turned to me and said, "At 47 years old, life is too short."

TRUISMS

1. Live like a squirrel.
2. Develop a personal budget and live within it.
3. Develop a Business Plan.
4. Get to know your local banker.
5. Tell everyone you know that you are in business and ask for referrals.
6. Get involved in your community.
7. The more personal your product or service is perceived to be, the more personal your marketing has to be.
8. Put a first class stamp on your mailing. Do not use third class mail rates.
9. Utilize an existing expertise and build a business based on your current skills.
10. Keep separate checkbooks for your personal and your business use.
11. Your tax accountant should be your most trusted financial advisor.
12. It is usually to your advantage to elect the largest insurance deductible available.

ENTREPRENEUR:

A PERSON WHO WORKS 12 HOURS A DAY TO AVOID A 8 HOUR A DAY JOB.

INDEX

ORDER FORM

Sherwood Publishing
1906 Canyonwood Ct.
Valrico, Fl 33594
(813) 685-3932

Send To:

____

____

____

Phone: (   )

Profiles In Independence:
Starting A Home-Based Business   **$ 14.95** ___________

Number of Copies: _________ = ___________

Shipping:
Book Rate: $2.00 for the first book
$.75 for each additional book.
(Shipping may take 3-4 weeks)
Air Mail: $3.50 per book   ___________

Florida Residents add 6.5% sales tax ___________

Total: ___________

PAYMENT:
Visa____ Mastercard____
Check____

Card Number:________________
Name on Card:________________

Exp. Date___/___

FROM

____

____

____

Stamp

TO:

Sherwood Publishing
1906 Canyonwood Court
Valrico, Fl 33594